THE EGYPTIAN MAU'S CHILDREN

History of the breed cat

Collection Animaux

THE EGYPTIAN MAU'S CHILDREN

History of the breed cat

La loi du 11 mars 1957 n'autorisant, aux termes des alinéas 2 et 3 de l'article 41, d'une part, que les « copies ou reproductions strictement réservées à l'usage privé du copiste et non destinées à une utilisation collective » et d'autre part, que les analyses et les courtes citations dans un but d'exemple et d'illustration, « toute représentation ou reproduction intégrale, ou partielle, faites sans le consentement de l'auteur ou de ses ayants droit ou ayants cause est illicite » (alinéa 1° de l'article 40). Cette reproduction ou représentation, par quelque procédé que ce soit, constituerait donc une contrefaçon sanctionnée par les articles 425 et suivants du code pénal.

This book is sold subject to the condition that it shall not, by the way of trade or otherwise, be lent, resold, hired out, or otherwise circulated without the publisher's prior consent in any form of binding or cover other than that in which it is published and without a similar condition including this condition being imposed on the subsequent purchaser and without limiting the rights under copyright reserved above, no part of this publication may be reproduced, stored in or reproduced into a retrieval system or transmitted in any form or by any means (electronic, mechanical, photocopying, recording or otherwise), without the prior permission of both the copyright owner and the above-mentioned publisher of this book.

Copyright Didier Hallépée
2011

THE EGYPTIAN MAU'S CHILDREN

History of the breed cat

Same author, Carrefour du Net publisher, paper books

"Le chat mau égyptien", 2009
"Citations et proverbes chats et chiens", 2009
"Mot à mau, les pensées du chat mau", 2010
"Pensées Royales Canines, les pensées du King Charles", 2010
"Les enfants du chat mau – histoire du chat de race", 2011
"Mon chat m'a dit, mon chien m'a dit", 2011

"L'univers de la monétique", 2009
"Le Sepa, l'espace des paiements en euro", 2009
"Qualité et sécurité informatique, les méthodes CMPI et CMSI", 2009
"La sécurité NFC", 2011
"La sécurité des systèmes embarqués", 2011

Same author, Carrefour du Net publisher, ebooks
"A ma fille", 2011
"Secrets de chat", 2011
"Secrets de chien", 2011
"Sudoku-neko volume 1", 2011
"Sudoku-neko volume 2", 2011
"Sudoku-neko volume 3", 2011
"Djambi, l'échiquier de Machiavel, *suivi du Sabacc*", 2011
"Le jeu de go", 2011
"Mon chat m'a conté", 2011
"Mon chien m'a conté", 2011
"Mon coq m'a conté", 2011
"Les secrets de Bastet, précis de génétique féline", 2011

Same author, Carrefour du Net publisher, in English
"The Egyptian Mau cat", 2011
"The Egyptian Mau children – story of the breed cat", 2011
"My cat told me, my dog told me", 2011
"Mau Mews (photo-comic)", 2011
"King Barks (photo-comic)", 2011
"Cat Secrets", 2011
"Dog Secrets", 2011
"Sudoku-neko volume 1", 2011
"Sudoku-neko volume 2", 2011
"Sudoku-neko volume 3", 2011
"CMPI, Managing and Mastering Computer Projects", 2009

Same author, Carrefour du Net publisher, in Italian
"I figli del gatto mau – storia del gatto di razza", 2011

To Isabelle, Leia and Jacen, with all my love.

to Doctor Giuseppe Mazza, photographer and scientific journalist thanks to whom I wrote this book whose texts are used on his animal web encyclopedia http://www.photomazza.com

to Doctor Giuliano Russini, author of the wonderful text about felidae for Giuseppe Mazza web site http://www.photomazza.com/?Mammiferi-Felidae-archivio&lang=en

to Josette Stouder, Mario Beltramini, René Stouder and Susana Franke who translated these texts into Italian, English and Spanish

To all my friends breeders with whom I share the love of the breed cat.

To all cat fanciers who know that a cat doesn't need to be a breed cat to be the most marvellous companion.

Most of the pictures come from de Wikipedia. They are under Creative Commons Paternity license or in the public domain.

Other pictures are the property of their author.

Meet the author on his forum 'Fondcombe writers' http://forum.fondcombe.com

CLASSIFICATION OF THE BREED CATS

The categories

The classification of breed cats does not follow biological or zoological rules. It has been done in function of the needs of feline shows. This classification rests upon the standards set up by the great feline associations and may differ from one association to another.

Thus it is that the cats of breed are classified into categories which compete separately in shows. The categories are based on the length of the hair.

They are:
- Long hair cats
- Medium-long hair cats
- Short hair cats

The Persian and all its varieties are considered as long hair cats.

The breeds of naked cats are classified in the short hair category.

The American associations such as CFA and TICA classify long and short hair cats in a single category.

Some associations, like FIFé, classify the Siamese and the Oriental in a different category.

As a principle, the long or short hair varieties should be classified as different races in separate categories. But they are often classified as varieties of one and the same race, into the category corresponding to the oldest variety.

So, the **Exotic Shorthair**, the short hair variety of the **Persian**, is often classified with the Persians in the long hair cat category.

Similarly, the **Somali**, the medium-long haired variety of the **Abyssinian**, is often classified with the Abyssinians in the short haired cat category.

Finally, marriages between long hair and short hair varieties are allowed in some breeds. These marriages generate, in particular, short haired specimens carrying the long hair gene. They are called variants. Some associations do not make any distinction between these variants and the short hair varieties. Others classify them with the long hair specimens and make them compete as such....

The notion of breed

Photo D. Hallépée

The domestication of the cat started in the Pharaohs' Egypt. Its function as protector of the harvests did seduce the Egyptians who worshipped it through the goddess Bastet. The mummies of cats found in Bubastis show us that by that time the cat had already existed in various colors. However, all representations of cats on frescoes and papyri show us a reddish-brown cat with a fur spotted with black dots. Similar cats are still found along the Egyptian roads, where they are called Pharaoh's cats. It can be thought that these cats were under the patronage of the pharaohs and formed the élite of the cats of that time. It was probably the first step towards the notion of cat breed. Nowadays, their descendants are called Egyptian Maus.

In spite of prohibitions, cats were exported from Egypt. So, they multiplied in Asia, following the Silk Road. They also followed the route of caravans, installing themselves all over North Africa. Embarked on vessels where they excelled in fighting against rats, they then populated the coastal areas of the Mediterranean, settled down in Rome and from there spread all over Europe, reaching, later, the New World. During their slow migration, they maintained their original diversity even if acquiring at times some specific characters for adapting to habitats very different from the banks of the Nile.

During all that period, the cat remained a utility animal taking advantage of its collaboration with men.

In the seventeenth century, a few travelers brought from Turkey some cats with a long and silky hair, thus causing a real enthusiasm. That type of cat was called Turkish Angora. This was probably the first time that a type of cat was identified and given a specific denomination. This infatuation had another consequence: it was the beginning of a slow process which turned the cat into a pleasure animal, a process which got faster during the twentieth century thanks to improvement in the struggle against rodents, a process which reduced its role as a utility animal.

It was during the nineteenth century that the first beauty contests for felines were organized (Crystal Palace, London, 1871). Thanks to these feline shows, fanciers began to produce original cats and the notion of a breed cat did then come to life.

At Crystal Palace there were only British cats and Persians. The other breeds came afterwards. At the beginning, the recognized breeds were very few and the criteria defining a breed were rather rudimentary. So, a Persian was just a long hair cat, and an Abyssinian was a cat with a coat with ticking.

By the twentieth century, the cat really attained its standing as pleasure animal and the world of feline shows got organized. Several breeders aiming at producing cats with original beauty wanted the cat they bred to be recognized as different. Thus it was that the different breeds of cats became progressively codified. The creation of feline organizations allowed structuring the feline shows and codifying the different breeds through the standards describing them and the pedigrees tracing their descent. Nowadays, new breeds are regularly created, evidencing one or another characteristic which is not shared with the other breeds.

The different breeds are defined by means of a standard. This one describes the morphology and the colors which characterize the breed considered. The art of breeding lies in producing cats as close as possible to the ideal type defined for the breed.

In order to be a breed cat, a cat must correspond to the standard and justify a descent from cats of the same breed through a pedigree.

For the recent breeds, it is possible to admit a cat without a pedigree provided it is deemed in conformity to the standard of the breed. These cats are inscribed in a register of specific origin called RIEX (experimental registry). Its descendants are also inscribed in the same registry and do not fully become cats of breed until the fourth generation.

As for the new breeds, they are at first recognized in an experimental way and inscribed in a book of origin called RIA. The standard of the breed is defined and when there is a sufficient number of such cats, the breed is finally recognized.

The definition of breeds

Photo D. Hallépée

Every breed is defined on the basis of specific morphological and genetic characteristics. Some of them may appear casually in the feline population and give some of these subjects the appearance of breeds defined as above, but this does not turn them into cats of breed.

Some breeds are defined at first by the appearance of a particular genetic characteristic in a particular breed: curly hair, folded ears, pompom tail, short legs, nakedness , etc...

As a principle, crossings between breeds are not authorized: the kittens obtained in this way are ordinary house cats, even if they have a wonderful character and are considered by their masters as having a very great beauty... Nevertheless, in the recent breeds, some marriages are authorized in order to get the breed stabilized without being obliged to go in for excessive consanguinity.

In several instances, the same breed can decline into short hair and (middle-) long hair. At times, these two variations carry different names. According to feline organizations, they may be considered either as different breeds or as different varieties of the same breed.

Some breeds are not recognized by all feline organizations.

The standards determining a breed differ from one organization to another. They also evolve with the passing of time ….

The varieties

Photo D. Hallépée

Every breed is subdivided into varieties. They permit cats homogeneously alike to compete together in order that comparison between them may be made on the basis of objective criteria, which themselves are based on standards instead of taste-based criteria.

The main subdivision into varieties is based on color. In some races, a very great number of colors is accepted. In others, the number of colors is very limited. Some colors are not accepted by all feline organizations.

Another subdivision into varieties rests upon the length of the hair.

Often, when there are short- and longhaired varieties (at times under different breed names), marriages are authorized. As the long hair gene is recessive, there appear short hair kittens carriers of the long hair gene and likely to generate long hair descendants. These cats are called variants and are identified as such in order to facilitate the work of selection inside the breed. The following rules are applied in the relevant unions:
  Short hair + short hair = short hair
  Long hair + long hair = long hair

Short hair + long hair = variant
Short hair + variant = variant
Long hair + variant = variant or long hair
Variant + variant = variant or long hair

The variants are not identified as such in all origin books.

Listing of the breeds

Photo AIME

Long hair category

Long hair breeds
> PERSIAN
> CHINCHILLA (PERSIAN of the division TIPPED)
> HIMALAYAN (PERSIAN of the division POINTED)
> EXOTIC SHORTHAIR

For ordinary mortals (who, poor humans, have only one life, unlike cats), there are cats with long hair and cats with short hair. On the other hand, some feline associations, such as CFA, have adopted this point of view.

In any case, the hair of the Persian (awn hair) is really the longest among the breeds with long hair. Furthermore, the mid-sized hair (guard hair) is abundant, which increases the thickness of the coat and gives it a fluffy appearance in a well groomed Persian. This is the reason why some feline associations consider long hair cats (Persians) and middle-long hair cats (the others) separately.

Several breeding generations have given the Persian its particular flat-faced look which cannot be mistaken with any other one.

And this very specific look is also found in its shorthaired variety, the Exotic shorthair.

Traditionally, the Exotic shorthair is judged along with the Persians with whom it shares the same standard, instead of being judged with shorthair cats.

Other colors of Persians use specific denominations: Chinchilla, Himalayan and Cameo.

Medium long hair category

<u>Breeds exclusively with medium-long hair</u>
- TURKISH ANGORA
- MAINE COON
- NORWEGIAN
- TURKISH OF LAKE OF VAN
- BIRMAN
- SIBERIAN
- YORK CHOCOLATE

In the medium-long hair breeds, the midsized hair (guard hair) is roughly of the same size as the longest one (awn hair), which gives a fur adhering better to the body, thus increasing the resemblance of these breeds to the short hair ones.

Furthermore, this ensures the impermeability of the fur and has granted the Turkish Angora and the Turkish Van the reputation of swimming cats.

Moreover, in most of the breeds with medium-long hair, the down hair is almost inexistent, which gives them a fur which does not get tangled.

<u>Breeds both with medium-long hair or short hair</u>
- AMERICAN BOBTAIL
- AMERICAN CURL
- BRITISH
- JAPANESE BOBTAIL
- KURILIAN BOBTAIL
- LAPERM
- MUNCHKIN
- PIXIE BOB
- SELKIRK REX
- SELKIRK STRAIGHT
- TONKINESE

The short hair breeds are the most numerous. Each one has its lovers and they all have the unmistakable advantage of a fur easy to maintain.

Nevertheless, long hair furs go on seducing by their beauty... And some breeders have asked themselves at times "what would this cat be like with long hair...?"

Some have made the decision of introducing the long hair gene by means of crossings, then have selected the specimens obtained in such a way in order to find the characteristics of the original breed. That's why several shorthaired breeds include a longhaired variety, under the same name or with a different one.

In some breeds, legend reports a spontaneous mutation. In any case, it is through the selection work of breeders that we have got the necessary quality by which the longhaired variety can be recognized.

Breeds having a short hair correspondence

    SOMALI
    TIFFANY
    CALIFORNIAN REX
    CYMRIC
    SHIRAZI
    ORIENTAL LONGHAIR
    MANDARIN
    NEBELUNG
    BALINESE
    HIGHLAND FOLD
    HIGHLAND STRAIGHT

Short hair category

The cat's fur is composed of three types of hair: guard hair (the longest hair, those composing the coat), awn hair (midsize hair forming an isolating layer) and down hair (or undercoat).

Down hair and awn hair have an even color. Awn hair is formed by colored bands which give the fur its different tints.

Some specific genes modify the structure of the hair. The selection of the cats presenting these genetic particularities has made the creation of specific breeds possible.

The recessive form of gene R is responsible for the absence of awn hair. The cat therefore has only the shortest hair (down and guard hair), which is short and wavy. This gene is typical of the Cornish Rex.

The recessive form of gene Re gives a short length to the three types of hair which, in effect, are wavy. This gene is characteristic of the Devon Rex.

The dominant form of gene Se makes the hair curly and abundant. It is characteristic of the Selkirk Rex.

The dominant form of gene Wh makes the hair curly and hard to the touch. This gene is typical of the American Wirehair.

The recessive form of gene hr is responsible for the almost total absence of the three types of hair. This gene is characteristic of the Sphynx.

Also, the dominant form of gene Hp is responsible for the almost total absence of the three types of hair. This gene is characteristic of the Donskoy and the Peterbald.

Breeds exclusively with short hair

- AMERICAN SHORTHAIR
- AMERICAN WIREHAIR
- BENGAL
- BOMBAY
- AMERICAN BURMESE
- CALIFORNIA SPANGLED
- CEYLON
- CHARTREUX
- CHAUSIE
- DEVON REX
- DONSKOY
- EUROPEAN SHORTHAIR
- GERMAN REX
- HAVANA BROWN
- KORAT
- OCICAT
- PETERBALD
- RAGDOLL
- SAVANNAH

SINGAPURA
SNOWSHOE
SOKOKE
SPHYNX
THAI

Breeds both with medium-long hair and short hair

AMERICAN BOBTAIL
AMERICAN CURL
BRITISH
JAPANESE BOBTAIL
KURILIAN BOBTAIL
LAPERM
MUNCHKIN
PIXIE BOB
SELKIRK REX
SELKIRK STRAIGHT
TONKINESE

Breeds with a long hair correspondence

EXOTIC SHORTHAIR

Breeds having a medium-long hair correspondence

ABYSSINIAN
ASIAN
ENGLISH BURMESE
BURMILLA
CORNISH REX
MANX
EGYPTIAN MAU
ORIENTAL
RUSSIAN
SIAMESE
SCOTTISH FOLD
SCOTTISH STRAIGHT

The correspondences between breeds

PERSIAN (LH)	EXOTIC SHORTHAIR (SH)
ABYSSINIAN (SH)	SOMALI (MLH)
ASIAN (SH)	TIFFANY (MLH)
BURMESE ANGLAIS (SH)	TIFFANY (MLH)
BURMILLA (SH)	TIFFANY (MLH)
CORNISH REX (SH)	CALIFORNIAN REX (MLH)
MANX (SH)	CYMRIC (MLH)
EGYPTIAN MAU (SH)	SHIRAZI (MLH)
ORIENTAL (SH)	MANDARIN (MLH)
RUSSIAN (SH)	NEBELUNG (MLH)
SIAMESE (SH)	BALINAIS (MLH)
SCOTTISH FOLD (SH)	HIGHLAND FOLD (MLH)
SCOTTISH STRAIGHT (SH)	HIGHLAND STRAIGHT (MLH)

A – LONG HAIR CATEGORY

PERSIAN
CHINCHILLA (PERSIAN of the division TIPPED)
HIMALAYAN (PERSIAN of the division POINTED)
EXOTIC SHORTHAIR

PERSIAN & EXOTIC SHORTHAIR

Photo Cindy See

History

<u>The Persian</u>

During the sixteenth century, the European aristocracy became fond of the Turkish Angora, a new cat from the Middle East, whose fur and character won their hearts.

It was at the same epoch that the cat began to assume its place as a pleasure animal, abandoning courtyards for the halls of villas.

During the nineteenth century, the English crossed the Turkish Angora with the British, which had a very attractive rounded face. Thus it was that the Persian came to life, a new breed with a name reminding one of its middle-eastern origins. It was presented alongside the British on the occasion of the first feline show at Crystal Palace on 1871.

The Persian became soon very familiar, so much so at it caused the Turkish Angora to be forgotten for many decades. The popularity of the breed quickly conquered the USA which went on with the work of selection the English had started. The Americans went further ahead, rounding the Persian even more and pushing its flat-faced appearance to the extreme.

Since then, the work of breeders has permitted the various colors to be created which are now admitted.

The Exotic Shorthair
The Exotic Shorthair came into existence in the USA during the fifties. At the beginning, it was just a matter of ameliorating the American Shorthair by giving it the rounded face of the Persian. The outcome was the short hair version of the Persian.

Temper

The Persian and the Exotic Shorthair are calm cats, easy to handle, home-loving. At times, they are described as plush. However, outside siesta time, each also shows the character of an authentic feline, of an explorer, of a very good hunter and a good tree-climber, capable of defending its own territory from all intruders.

The fur of the Persian requires regular grooming so as to emphasize its beauty and avoid hair entanglement. This regular grooming and its rounded face make this cat an ideal companion for anyone in need of human affection.

When we see a Persian at a show, it's a real ball of fluffy hair framing a round face. Such a result can be obtained only with a very regular grooming and an intensive preparation just before the show (shampooing, drying up, dressing, etc.). When we wander through the corridors at a show, it is not rare to see a breeder turning his Persian in all the directions so as to get its hair puffed up. Reaching the highest places on the podium results from several hours of preparation work.

The Exotic Shorthair has inherited its character from the Persian. Its shorthaired fur requires much less grooming.

Part of its character is connected to its color.

Photo Lajorna

Standard

Round and massive, the head shows a wide dome-like skull. The face is round with a sweet expression and a well rounded bone framework. The cheeks are wide and powerful, with prominent and full cheek-bones. Viewed from the side, the nose and the chin are aligned on the same vertical plane.

The nose is wide and very short, with sufficiently open nostrils so that breathing is not disturbed. The stop, well marked and deep, must be situated between the eyes, ideally in the middle, never higher than the upper line of the eyes and never below the lower line.

The muzzle must be round, wide and full, which is evidence of a perfect occlusion of the mandibles. The chin is strong.

The eyes are rounded, big and well spaced out; the eyes have a sweet look. Their color, which is very intense, must be in accordance with that of the mantle.

The ears are almost round, not too open at the base, small and sufficiently apart from each other, placed in such a way that they do not alter the roundness of the head. The Persian's inner ears are very bushy. The neck is thick, massive and short, the head seems to be built into the shoulders.

The body is cobby and massive, with rounded shoulders and hips of the same width. The back is straight. The chest is broad. The thorax must be muscular without any sign of obesity.

The legs are short, robust, strong and very straight. The feet are round and solid.

The tail is short, thick at the base, ending in a rounded tuft, but proportioned with the length of the body. In the case of the Persian, the tail is very thick.

Coat and texture of the Persian: long all over the body, shoulders included, the fur is thick, delicate and silky. An abundant undercoat makes the whole voluminous. The collar, much developed, continues down to between the front legs and under the belly.

Coat and texture of the Exotic Shorthair: thick and pleasant to the touch, the fur stands up on the body thanks to the thickness of its down hair. Slightly longer than that of other breeds of short hair cats, it must not however be so long as to lie on the body or to wave.

Short hair variety

The short hair variety of the Persian is called Exotic Shorthair.

Authorized crossings

Persian x Persian
Persian x Exotic Shorthair
Exotic Shorthair x Exotic Shorthair

Coat

All colors are recognized for the Persian and the Exotic Shorthair.

The colors are usually grouped in divisions in order to facilitate comparison during a show.

Solid division

This division includes all the solid colors.

Tabby division

This division gathers all tabby patterns, that is, those showing a pattern. There are four tabby patterns recognized for Persians and Shorthairs: the ticked pattern, the spotted pattern, the mackerel pattern and the blotched pattern.

Silver/smoke division

The undercoat is silvery in the silver and smoke cats. In the silver or smoke Persian and Exotic Shorthair, the silver base must be uniformly spread all over the body, head, legs and tail included. It must be between 1/4 and 1/3 of the length of the hair at its base. The Persian and the smoke Exotic Shorthair must have white hair in their ears.

Tipped (Chinchilla) division

Tipping is a phenomenon giving the hair of the cat a white base while preserving the original color at the tip of the hair. Only the extremity of the hair is colored in the case of the tipped cat. For the Shaded Persian, the colored part extends up to a third of the hair. The Persians having these marks are called Chinchillas.

The hair is white in the Silver, golden in the Golden. The tabby marks do not appear.

Point division (Himalayan)

The colorpoint is the typical marking of the Siamese in which only the tips are colored.

Sepia is the typical marking of the Burmese which gives the body a pale color. Mink is the typical marking of the Tonkinese, which gives a light color on the body and a darker one on the extremities.

The Persians having these markings are called Himalayans.

In this division, there must be a clear contrast between the color of the points, which is as homogeneous as possible, and that of the body, which is uniform. The absence of ghost marks is desirable even if there is a tolerance for tabby cats.

Particolored division

Is considered as parti-colored every Persian or Exotic Shorthair part of whose fur is formed by white dots. The bicolor or tricolor pattern is considered as best when it is 25% to 50% white.

B – BREEDS EXCLUSIVELY WITH MEDIUM-LONG HAIR

TURKISH ANGORA
MAINE COON
NORWEGIAN
TURKISH OF LAKE OF VAN
BIRMAN
SIBERIAN
YORK CHOCOLATE

TURKISH ANGORA

Photo Pablo1964

History

The Turkish Angora appeared on the borders of Persia and Turkey, in the highlands (around Lake Van). Discovered by travelers, he was introduced in Europe in the seventeenth century. There was immediately a craze for this cat with long silky hair. Very popular in aristocratic circles in the eighteenth century, he was considered a royal gift. Very quickly, he conquered the world and took root in many countries. He was used to create the different longhair and semi-longhair breeds, especially the Persian. Then he was forgotten and almost disappeared from Europe in the nineteenth century. In the twentieth century, the Ankara Zoo launched a rescue program of the breed. According to legend, its scarcity was such that the export of this cat was punishable by death for a Turk or life imprisonment for a foreigner! In 1959, an American, Mrs. Charles Weed, rediscovered the Angora cat in Ankara Zoo and restarted his breeding in the United States.

The lake of Van

In the region of Lake Van, the natural food resources are so scarce that cats are forced to fish for their livelihood (the specific fish of this lake is called Darekh - a unique breed called chalcalburnus Taricha family Cyprinidae). And yet, at a height of 1,750 meters, the lake waters are icy cold. However, Turkish cats have no undercoat, which makes their fur waterproof (and also prevents it from tangling). This gave Turkish cats (Turkish Angora and Turkish Van) the reputation of swimming cats. In an apartment, if you want to relax in your bathtub, close the door...

darekh (chalcalburnus tarichi)

The quality of his fur and of his temper make him an exceptional cat. He is traditionally white with a special glance (blue, gold, copper or odd eyes). He also exists in various colors. Very playful, very talkative, he loves coiling around your neck as you walk about. He is very, very cuddly and will seduce you.

As in all breeds, blueyed homozygotous white subjects can be deaf. This is not specific either to the subjects with blue eyes, nor to the Angora. Although it makes these cats even more cuddly, breeders avoid this risk by crossing regularly white subjects with colored subjects and avoiding the mating of homozygotous white cats together.

Photo Michel Pothier

Temper

The Turkish Angora is a graceful perfectly balanced cat, with a fine silky coat. When one handles it, one is surprised by its weight and the density of its muscles contrasting with the delicacy of its vaporous fur. Cats of this breed are intelligent, active and curious, and demand to be handled gently but firmly.

It's a race that will assert dominance over other races. With a strong personality, he is comfortable in show only when he finds himself faced with an authority more impressive than his.

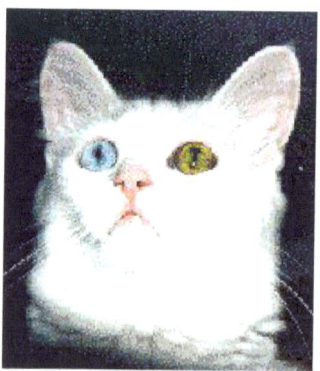

Photo Didier Hallépée

But mostly, he is a very affectionate cat who enjoys contact and caresses. His passion is curling up round the neck of his favorite two-legged creature, purring on and on while the latter goes on as well he can with his occupations.

Strong temper and tenderness: an amazing mixture.

His coat without an undercoat does not get tangled easily, maintenance is easy. However, the spring molt requires more frequent maintenance.

Photo Didier Hallépée

Standard

Small to medium compared to its body, the head is a smooth modified wedge. Seen from the side, the head shows two planes: one formed by a flattop head and forehead and the second by the line of the nose both meeting at an angle between the eyes.

Slightly rounded, the muzzle should be in continuation of the wedge, without a pinch. Firm chin.

Large, walnut-shaped, the eyes slightly slant upwards. Color of eyes should be in relationship with coat color.

Large, wide at base, the ears are set high on the head, vertical. They are slightly pointed, with abundant hair.

Photo Michel Pothier

Medium in length, the neck is slim and graceful.

Foreign in type, the body is long, slender and muscular. Chest is narrow and shoulders should be the same width as the hips. Firm musculature on a fine-boned structure.

Long, the hind legs are higher than the front legs.

Oval, the feet are small and delicate. Tufted toes are desirable.

Long, the tail is large at base, tapering to a narrow end and fully plumed.

Photo Catherine Niri

Semi-long, the coat is fine and silky, with little undercoat. Shining and shimmering, it is longer on ruff, britches, belly and tail. The coat can show slight waves on the stomach and noticeable seasonal variations.

Coat

The best known is the white Turkish Angora. Its color is due to gene W, which is responsible for the control of melanin, which is itself responsible for the expression of color. The heterozygotous Ww cat (called improperly "color bearer") can transmit color to its kittens. At birth, a heterozygotous white cat wears on the forehead a colored spot that will disappear with growth.

In homozygotous WW cats, the amount of melanin is lower. Thus, the color spot is not there (it's hard to know what colors are hidden by the white !). When the amount of melanin is low, the cat's eyes are blue. Too small a quantity of melanin has repercussions on the ear and then the cat may be deaf. Hence, the legend that all white cats with blue eyes are deaf.

Photo Didier Hallépée

To avoid deafness, breeders fight the low rate of melanin by crossing white angora and colored angora. Thus, the white kittens who will be born will be heterozygotous Ww and will not be deaf.

Melanin may be unevenly distributed, a white cat with blue eyes can have odd eyes, that is to say, one blue eye and the other a different color (green, amber or brown). In some cases, the cat may be deaf on the side of the blue eye.

A deaf cat is of course forbidden to enter a show. In some countries, all blue-eyed white cats are banned from shows, which is a little excessive as a method to fight against the risk of deafness.

MAINE COON

Photo Lengoma

History

After leaving the banks of the Nile and settling in Europe, the cat quite simply followed pioneers in the conquest of the New World, where it adapted to the different habitats available.

According to a folk tale, some of them crossed the depths of Maine forests together with raccoons, thus originating a feline big-sized species whose color recalled that of its ancestor. Clearly, this is impossible, but it is believed by some that this is where its name "Coon" comes from, a name which, later on, was prolonged into Maine Coon.

According to another legend, Marie-Antoinette, scared by the revolution, had thought of taking shelter in the United States. The lesson of Varennes had been understood, as her second flight was better organized. She was able to hand over her six Turkish Angoras to Capt. Clough in command of of the vessel she was to have joined. The flight never took place, and the Angoras found themselves alone in the house intended for the queen, close to the state of Maine. The Main Coon should be a descendant of these cats.

Another tale narrates that the Main Coon comes from the cats which travelled with the Vikings around the year 1000 during their explorations of the New World.

Whatever its origin may be, the Main Coon is a remarkable adaptation of a race of cats with semi-long hair to the specific conditions of the Maine forests, an adaptation which caused the changes necessary for them to take better advantage of their habitat, and made them the biggest of breed cats .

The first Maine Coon, Captain Jencks, was presented at the shows of Boston and New York in 1881. Little by little, the Maine Coon passed over the boundaries of the state and then fell into oblivion not to re-emerge from it until the fifties.

It was recognized as a breed in 1967.

The introduction of the Maine Coon in France dates from 1981, but the breed became popular in the early nineties only.

Temper

The Maine Coon is the biggest domestic cat. It can weigh as much as 11 kg (without being obese, of course).

Solidly built and with a rustic appearance, the Maine Coon is described as a gentle giant.

Very sociable, it likes kids and also other animals. It is a good hunter, playful, sporting and very affectionate towards its masters.

It is described also as a "cat-dog", being able to bring back a toy in order to have it thrown again. It is quite willing to go for a short walk on a leash. Males are clearly more imposing than females.

Photo Wikimaster97

Standard

The head is of a good size, both in length and width, with high salient cheek-bones. Seen from the side, the line of the nose forms a slightly concave bend without a stop. The skull is slightly rounded.

Seen from the front, the muzzle looks square, whilst, if seen from the side, it distinctly stands out from the skull and is never sharp or narrow. The nose, lips and the tip of the chin are aligned on the same vertical thus increasing the "square" impression of the muzzle. The chin is firm and powerful. The balance in the proportions between head and length of the muzzle is essential.

Big, slightly oval and wide apart , the eyes are set obliquely but may seem round when the cat is vigilant. All tones of green, golden, copper or yellow are accepted even if there is no relationship between the color of the eyes and that of the mantle. Blue or un-matching eyes are accepted in white cats.

Big, wide at the base, situated high on the head (see tolerances), the ears are separated from each other by a space equivalent to the width of the base of one ear. Moderately sharp, they are slightly bent outwards. They are thickly haired and lynx tips are desirable.

Medium sized, the neckline is muscular.

Long and powerful, the body is big, strong-muscled and with a broad chest. Rectangular, it must not, however, show any exaggeration which might harm the general balance.

Solid, with a powerful musculature and a strong bone frame, the paws are moderately high, and this increases the rectangular look of the body.
Big and round, with five fingers in front and four at back, the feet have important inter-digital hair.

Long, the tail must ideally reach the base of the scapula. Wide at the base, it is particularly well furnished with long hair, which forms soft locks, and it ends with a tip.

Short on shoulders and thighs, the fur gets gradually longer on the sides reaching its full length on the belly and the rear. Much valued under the throat, the collar does not spread on to the chest. The texture is silky but firm and falls naturally on each side of the body. The down-hair is thin. The length of the fur and the thickness of the down-hair vary depending on the seasons and a mantle clearly shorter in summer must not be penalized by judges

Coat

All colors, but chocolate, lilac, cinnamon and fawn.

NORWEGIAN

Photo Pieter Lanser

History

After having left the banks of the Nile, the domestic cat spread all over Europe. It even went very far up North, reaching Norway where it met a particularly unfriendly habitat to which it had to adapt. Thus it was that it developed naturally a thick fur for fighting cold.

During the eighth century, Vikings spread all over Europe, reaching the most remote places of the Mediterranean. Some authors think that they may have carried home with them some specimens of long hair cats from the Caspian or the Black Seas. In this way, the Turkish Angora might have something to do with the history of the Norwegian cat. It may have been at the origin of the legend of the big white cats drawing the cart of Freyia, the goddess of fertility and love.

It is possible that these two origins joined together forming over the centuries a cat particularly suitable for the cold of the North.

The Norwegian cat as described around 1550 by Peter Clausson Friis. Since 1930 some breeders have taken an interest in preserving the originality of this cat and in getting its recognition. The breed was recognized in 1972.

The Norwegian is also known under the name of Skogkatt.

Photo Carl-Johan Aberger

Temper

The Norwegian is a cat high on its paws and this prevents contact of its abdomen with the cold of snow . Its rear paws are longer than the fore ones, a specificity favourable to running and jumping... When an adult, the male can reach 6-7 kg f in weight, the female is smaller with a weight of 4 kg.

A semi-longhair cat, it is equipped with woolly down-hair and a water-repellent outer coat, an originality which cannot be found in any other breed.

An abundant collarette encircles the head and gives the cat a very particular look.

It has qualities as a climber and jumper and excels in climbing up trees, from which it comes down with its head first, a specificity of the breed. It has also great qualities as a hunter. Its size allows this cat to attack big preys, such as hares, turkeys and geese.

It has a particularly pleasant temper, is very much of a "glue pot", very calm, of great temperamental stability. Calm, but always present, it much enjoys the company of the different members of the family, kids, other cats and dogs.

Standard

Of medium size, the head is the shape of an equilateral triangle. The upper head and the forehead, slightly rounded, are followed by a straight nose, without a curve or stop.

The muzzle has no pinch; the chin is firm.

Big, almond-shaped, the eyes are set rather obliquely and give the cat an attentive lively expression. All colors of eyes are authorized, whatever the coat color may be.

Medium to big, the ears are well open at the base, slightly pointed at the top and placed on the extension of the triangle. Seen in profile, they point forward. Lynx tips are desirable but not compulsory. The internal fur of the ears extends up to their outer edge.

Muscular, the neckline is of medium size.

The body is rather long, powerful and strong, with a robust bone frame and a full broad chest.

Rather high, the paws are strong-muscled and have solid bones.

Big and round, the feet have tufts of hairs between the toes.

Long, thick at the base and bushy, the tail is ideally as long as the body.

The coat is double. Long, water-repellent and glossy outer coat hairs cover a woolly down-hair, giving an impression of heaviness and depth.

The collarette is formed by long hairs starting from the back of the ears and by a very abundant frill.

The collarette and the rumps are bulky and formed only by down-hair.

The quality of the fur is much more important than the color.

Coat

All colors, except those based on chocolate, lilac, cinnamon and fawn.

BIRMAN

Photo grapheum.de

History

According to legend, a long time ago in Burma there was an old monk taking care of a temple dedicated to a golden goddess with sapphire eyes. This monk had a cat named Sinh. One day, the temple was attacked and the monk killed. Sinh jumped on to the head of its master and looked at the statue of the goddess straight in the eyes. Its eyes became then sapphires and its skin golden, like the goddess, but its paws remained white, like the hair of the monk on which they were lying. After a few days, the cat died of a broken heart. Then it was that all the cats of the temple underwent a metamorphosis and became the sacred Birman cats.

Much later on, a couple of sacred cats was stolen in the temple of Lao Tseu and reached France in 1920.

Those who do not believe in legends say that the sacred Birman cat was born in France in 1920 from the crossing of a white-gloved Siamese cat with a Persian.

Whatever happened, the Second World War was then raging, decimating both stray cats and domestic cats. After the war, there was just one pair of sacred Birman cats left alive, Orloff & Xénia de Kaaba. All present sacred Birman cats descend from them.

Temper

The sacred Birman cat is an affectionate cat, sweet and playful.

Its semi-long hair and its colorpoint pattern give it an elegance which is enhanced by the gloves of its four paws.

To raise breed cats means to work on living creatures and to accept the unforeseeable. Whatever a breeder's efforts may be, Madame Nature has the last word. As far as the sacred Birman cat is concerned, getting a white gloving and its transmission to the descendants are rather unpredictable. The corresponding genetic criteria are not yet mastered and only the skill (and luck) of the breeder permit him or her to get a very beautiful gloving.

Photo Claudia Zaino

Standard

Of medium size, the head is wide, triangular with rounded contours. The cheeks are full. The forehead is slightly rounded. The profile line is continued by a slightly concave change of direction at the level of the eyes. Without a stop, the nose is Roman, that is, curved.

Medium-sized, the muzzle is broad, without a pinch. The chin is strong.

Great, almost rounded, the eyes are set wide apart and the blue color is the most intense possible.

The ears are medium-sized, almost as wide as high. Spaced out the width of an ear, they have a rounded tip. The interior is quite hairy.

Of medium size, the neck is muscular.

The Sacred Birman has a long powerful body, bulky, with a straight regular back.

Of medium height, the paws have a robust bone structure and a good musculature.

The feet are big, round and solid.

Of medium size, the tail is proportioned to the body.

Semi-long, the coat is very silky. Short on the face, it gradually gets longer from the cheeks down to a collar which is very much appreciated in males. The coat is long on the back and the sides. The undercoat is not abundant and light. The hair may curl tightly on the belly. Note: seasonal changes must be kept in mind when judging the length of its coat.

The fore-paws, front and back, have white gloves ending in a right line, ideally at the junction between the foot and the paw. The rearpaws have white fore-gloves extending to the back of the paw and ending in a point from half to three-quarters of the heels (spurs). Regularity between the heights of fore-gloves and rear gloves is desirable.

The pads are pink and/or of a color corresponding to the base color of the cat.

Coat

All colors, colorpoint pattern.

SIBERIAN

Photo Cybercop2000

History

On settling in Europe, the cat pushed his explorations to the Urals and beyond. Thus he could meet the wildcat of Siberian forests. From this encounter grew an original breed, the Siberian.

As everywhere in Europe, the nobility became fascinated with some breeds of cats and many were the people who had Siamese, Burmese, Angoras. The meeting of these cats with the Siberian offered the latter with a wide range of colors.

From Peter the Great onwards, the cat was appreciated and protected. But the originality of the Siberian was only belatedly recognized.

With the perestroika in the 1980s, the Russians became interested in breeding cats. And with the fall of the Berlin wall, November 9, 1989, the Siberian cat left Russia to discover the western countries.

Temper

The Siberian cat is a large cat (6 to 10 kg for males, 3.5 kg to 7 kg for females). It's a quiet strong animal that can be very active and energetic, getting along well with other animals and very attached to its owner.

Curious, intelligent, he needs company and does not like being left alone. Young at heart, he repeats the behavior that caused the laughter of his master.

To survive, the Siberian cat needed to have access to domestic heat . For such access not to be refused to him, he had to adapt and become sociable and clean, two qualities he has kept until now.

It is probable that these constraints made for natural selection and turned him into a specifically allergen free cat (Fel d1 protein levels very low in saliva).

Photo Arbilad

Standard

The shape of the head is a modified wedge, large with rounded contours. Viewed from the front, the cheekbones are neither high set nor prominent. The skull is broad and almost flat. Viewed from the side, the forehead is slightly round and continued by a slight curve between the eyes. The nose is medium in length and flat.

Round and strong, it must be without a pinch. Females often have a thinner muzzle than males. The chin is rounded without being protruding. Whiskers are long and thick.

Large, almost round, they are set at least one eye's width apart. Slightly slanted, without having an oriental look. All eye colors are accepted even if without any relationship with coat color, except in the colorpoints which have blue eyes.

Medium in size, large at base and set apart the width of an ear to an ear and a half. Seen from the side, they are slightly tilted forward. Round at the end, the ears have an important fur covering their base almost entirely. Abundant hair inside, lynx tips desirable.

Round and short, the neck is heavy-muscled.

The body is semicobby, massive, heavy and muscular, with a characteristic barrel-shaped appearance, due the to roundness of the ribs and the musculature. The back is arched and higher than the shoulders, the belly is firm.

Medium in length, the legs are sturdy and strong-muscled with substantial boning.

Big and rounded, the feet have abundant toe tufts.

Wide at the base, tapering to a blunt tip, the tail is thick and abundant. It should ideally reach the base of shoulder blades.

Semi-long to long, the Siberian's coat is made of three types of hair: guard, down and awn hair. The hair on the shoulders, the lower part of the chest and back should be coarse and shiny. Ruff goes from back of head down to chest. Abundant undercoat. The hair may thicken to curls on the belly, but a wavy coat is not characteristic. In parti-colours white is allowed in any amount and in all areas.

The overall appearance of the Siberian should reflect strength and power, balanced by a sweet expression.

Coat

All colors except those based on chocolate, lilac, cinnamon and fawn.

The colorpoint variety of Siberians is called Neva Masquerade.

TURKISH OF LAKE OF VAN

Photo Biseyli

History

Turkey is home to two natural breeds of cats: Turkish Angora and Turkish of Lake of Van. Turkish of Lake of Van is distinguished by its characteristic pattern: a white coat with colorful hat and tail, usually red.

The lake of Van

In the region of Lake Van, the natural food resources are so scarce that cats are forced to fish for their livelihood (the specific fish of this lake is called Darekh - a unique breed called chalcalburnus Taricha family Cyprinidae). And yet, at a height of 1,750 meters, the lake waters are icy. However, Turkish cats have no undercoat, which makes their fur waterproof (and also prevents it from tangling). This gave Turkish cats (Turkish Angora and Turkish of Lake of Van) the reputation of swimming cats. In an apartment, if you want to relax in your bathtub, close the door...

The harsh living conditions have made the Turkish cat of Lake of Van a very muscular animal, a force of nature. A long-haired cat, solidly built, he is perfectly adapted to the climatic variations of this rugged area.

He reaches full maturity around the age of three years.

darekh (chalcalburnus tarichi)

Temper

The Turkish of Lake of Van is a muscular well built cat, a perfectly balanced cat, with a fine silky coat. Cats of this breed are intelligent, active and curious, and demand to be handled gently but firmly.

It's a dominant breed with a strong temper. He is comfortable at shows only when he finds himself faced with an authority more impressive than his own. In this case, his attachment to his human companion appears in his waiting patiently beside the latter, should it be on the roof of a car, a coffee table or a show cage, despite the feline instinct that pushes cats to go out in a reckless exploration of the wide world.

He is a very affectionate cat who enjoys contact and caresses. The softness of his fur is reflected in his caress.

His coat without an undercoat does not often get tangled, maintenance is easy. However, the spring molt requires more frequent maintenance.

Photo Michel Pothier

Standard

Slightly longer than wide, the head, seen from the front, is triangle-shaped, with rounded contours. It is wider in males than in females. Cheekbones are high and slightly prominent. The
profile shows a slightly rounded forehead followed by a small curve between the eyes, leading to a nose curved slightly downward – not a Roman, however. –

The muzzle is neat, rounded and proportionate to the rest of the head, with a definite but not sharp pinch, that must be felt through the fur. The chin is round.

Large and expressive, the walnut-shaped eyes are set slightly obliquely. Preferably, eye color is blue, gold or odd-eyed, as uniform and intense as possible.

Medium to large, the ears are set fairly high on the head without being vertical. Wide at the base, with rounded tips, the inside hair is abundant.

Of medium size, muscular, with an abundant ruff when the cat is in its winter coat.

Long and powerful, the body is large and strong. The powerful round musculature can be felt through the coat. The chest is particularly developed, broad and open, the shoulders are broad and the ribcage is round (no slab sides). The shoulders are wider than the rump, especially in males.

Medium-long, the legs have a moderate bone structure but a very strong musculature.

They are neat and round, with tufted toes.

Medium in length, the bushy tail is a plume. The color of tail does not extend to hips, preferably.

Semi-long, the coat has a soft cashmere-like texture, with as little woolly undercoat as possible. Due to the extreme continental climate of his native region, the Turkish Van displays two distinctive coat lengths. The summer coat is almost short; only the tail, tummy and part of the britches indicate it is a semi-long-haired cat. Winter coat is a dense inextricable ball of fur, longer and thicker. Facial fur is short. Coat, especially on neck ruff and full tail, becomes more pronounced with age, mature males being quite impressive.

<u>Coat</u>

The Turkish Van displays a typical pattern in which, ideally, color is confined to top of head and tail. Color on head should be divided into two patches on forehead and back of skull, as symmetrical as possible and divided by a white inverted V up to the forehead. Ears are white. Because of S gene, distribution of white being random even at homozygotous state , two or three color patches on the back and back of legs are allowed, if the amount of color of the entire body does not exceed 20%, head and tail included. Paw pads are pink. Some color spots are allowed if not too invasive.

Photo Michel Pothier

Originally, the Turkish Van was white with red patterns.

Today, all solid colors are accepted on the white coat, except those based on chocolate, lilac, cinnamon and fawn.

The white Turkish of Lake of Van is called Van Kedisi.

YORK CHOCOLATE

Photo Nickstein00

History

The York Chocolate is a semi-long cat of chocolate or lilac color, with or without white spots.

The breed was born with the casual appearance of a chocolate kitten in a litter of domestic cats at Janet Chiefari's in New York.

The breed was named York Chocolate in homage to its city of origin and its color. It was recognized in 1992.

Temper

It is a gay, energetic and playful cat who tends to develop a more exclusive relationship with one member of the family.

Standard

Almost round when seen from the front, the head is medium-sized. Seen in profile, the forehead is slightly convex and there is, without any interruption, a slight concave slope between the forehead and the nose. The latter is straight or slightly curved.

Of medium length, the muzzle is neither pointed nor rounded. The chin is firm.

The eyes, oval, are big and well open. They can be gold or green. Blue eyes or of different colors (one eye is blue and the other green or gold) are accepted in the part-color. Ears: as high as broad at the base, they are situated at equal distance from the sides and the summit of the head. They are bushy.

Quite long, the neckline may seem shorter than it really is, due to the thickness of the fur.

Of semi-foreign format, the body is both elegant and muscular.

The paws, long, are thin but with a strong musculature.

The feet, rounded, are rather small.

Quite thick at the base, the tail is rather long, even if in proportion with the body.

Thin and silky, the fur is dense but with very little down-hair. Short and irregular on the shoulders, it gets longer gradually on the sides and reaches its full length on the belly and the knickers. There may be a ruff depending on the season. The tail is bushy.

Coat

The only two accepted colors are chocolate and lilac, which must be as deep and uniform as possible. The proportion of white in the part-colors goes from one third to half of the surface of the cat. The kittens may have some tabby marks (ghost marks) or a slight coloration of the hair resembling some tipping.

C – BREEDS BOTH WITH MEDIUM-LONG AND SHORT HAIR

Breeds both with medium-long hair or short hair

AMERICAN BOBTAIL
AMERICAN CURL
BRITISH
JAPANESE BOBTAIL
KURILIAN BOBTAIL
LAPERM
MUNCHKIN
PIXIE BOB
SELKIRK REX
SELKIRK STRAIGHT
TONKINESE

AMERICAN BOBTAIL

Photo Klarissae

History

The American Bobtail is a breed of cat native to the United States where it appeared following a genetic mutation characterized by the near absence of a tail.

The first specimens were discovered in Arizona by the Sanders family. The breed has been recognized since 1989.

The American Bobtail comes in two varieties : shorthair and longhair.

Temper

There are several types of tail:
- Snag: 2-8 vertebrae strongly deformed and glued together. It is often straight or slightly curved downwards.

- Spiral: 5-10 vertebrae forming a spiral or a hook. This type of tail is the most sought after.
- Whip: 5-10 vertebrae carried erect and measuring approximately ⅔ of the size of a normal tail.
- Delayed: 5-7 vertebrae starting normally (right) and ending with a hook. This type of tail is considered a fault.

The American Bobtail is affectionate, moderately active and emotional but not aggressive. Patient with children, he accepts the presence of a dog.

Standard

The head is broad with strong jaws and no flat plane. Viewed from the side, the nose shows a slight indentation between the eyes but there can be a small stop. The cheeks are full, the chin firm.

The muzzle is as long as wide with clearly defined whisker pads.

Large and wide, oval in shape, the eyes are set at a slant to the base of the ear. Eye color should be as uniform as possible.

Medium in size, the ears are wide at base, wide-open and set rather low. They are slightly rounded with lynx tips and abundant hair inside.

The neck looks short in proportion to the body because of the strong musculature and coat density.

Semi-cobby in type, the athletic powerful body is slightly longer than high. The flanks are broad, the back is straight. The chest is full and the hips are strong. Males should be more strongly built, with broad shoulders and a muscular appearance. Females, too, should be sinewy, while preserving feminine elegance.

Well-proportioned to the body, the legs have substantial boning and arestrongly muscled. Back legs should be longer than front legs.

Large and round.

Naturally short and flexible, the tail is from 2.5 to 10 cm (1" to 4") long (actual bone, hair not included) and may extend to the hock, but not past it.

Shorthair: medium-short coat, slightly shaggy with slightly longer hair on ruff, britches, belly and tail. Noticeable seasonal changes.

Longhair coat: semi-long coat, dense, shaggy, with abundant undercoat. Longer on ruff, britches, belly and tail. Tufted toes are desirable. Seasonal variations are admitted. Dense and resilient texture all year round.

The American Bobtail should give the impression of an active, alert, athletic cat, well- proportioned with a tail neither too long nor too short, so as not to affect its natural balance.

Authorized crossings

American Bobtail shorthair X American Bobtail shorthair
American Bobtail longhair X American Bobtail longhair
American Bobtail shorthair X American Bobtail longhair

Coat

All colors.

AMERICAN CURL

Photo Tanakawho

History

The American Curl is a breed of cat native to the United States where it appeared following a genetic mutation characterized by curved ears.

The first specimen was found in 1983 in the United States.

The breed was recognized in 1987.

The American Curl comes in two varieties: short hair and longhair.

Temper

The dominant form of Cu gene is responsible for curled ears, that is to say, ears bent backward. This gene is characteristic of the American Curl.

He is affectionate, emotional and moderately active but not aggressive. Patient with children, he accepts the presence of a dog.

Photo Wikipedia

Standard

The head is a medium triangle, longer than wide and without a flat plane. Viewed from the side, it displays rounded curves from the skull to a rather straight nose.

From the forehead onwards, the muzzle continues the head triangle, without a pinch and with rounded contours. The chin is firm.

Moderately large in proportion to the head, the eyes are walnut-shaped (oval on top and round at bottom). They are about one eye-width apart. All colors are accepted, if uniform: the more intense and brilliant, the better.

The ears are the distinctive and essential feature of the breed. They are curved out and back like a moon crescent in a 90° to 180° arc. The tip of each ear should not touch the back of the head or have an extreme curl that would close the ear and cause the tip to touch the back of the ear. Moderately large, they are set one ear width apart. Wide at base, they have firm cartilage from base to at least one third of height of the ear. The tip is flexible and rounded. Ears should have symmetrical curl andbe thickly haired inside. The specific shape of the American Curl's ears should not affect their natural movements when the cat is alert and attentive.

Rather long, the neck is slender and graceful.

Semi-foreign in type, the body is elegant and rectangular. Its length should be 1-1/2 times the height at the shoulders. The American Curl is a medium-sized cat, males often being larger than females. Musculature should be long and tonic. Bone structure is medium, neither heavynor fine.

Medium in length, in the right proportion to the body, the legs are straight, with medium bone structure.

The feet, medium in size, are rounded.

Thick at the base, the tail is as long as the body. It should be flexible.

Shorthair: short, silky, close-lying coat, with little undercoat. Tail coat should be as long as body coat.

Longhair: semi-long haired, finely textured, silky and flatlying, with minimal undercoat. The tail should be thick and abundant, with a full plume.

Authorized crossings

American Curl shorthair X American Curl shorthair
American Curl longhair X American Curl longhair
American Curl shorthair X American Curl longhair

Coat
All colors.

BRITISH

Photos Isabelle Bonte

History

The British is a breed of cats native to Great Britain.

It comes from the common English cat, a descendant of the cats which accompanied the Romans during their conquest and occupation of the British Isles. This was the first breed of shorthaired cats recognized in England in the XIXth century and it was showed at the Crystal Palace in 1871.

It has maintained its past robustness and solidity as a feral cat. It exists in several colors. Its character, full of sweetness, confirms the promises of its good-natured look.

It exists also in the longhair variety.

Temper

The British is a medium to bigsized cat, robust and powerful, of a well-rounded build. Its round, apple-shaped head has a sweet open expression, enhanced by its big eyes. Its round and short muzzle, its strong neck line, its powerful body with its very broad and round shoulders and hips, make it an imposing cat. It gives off a general impression of strength and of sweetness.

Photo Isabelle Bonte

Standard

The head is broad with wellrounded contours whatever the angle under which we look at it. The cheeks are full. The skull is rounded, sloping downward in a slightly concave curve. The nose is short and wide. A slight stop is admitted. Adult males have powerful jowls.

Both in a front view and seen in profile, the muzzle is inscribed in a clearly-defined circle with firm and full whisker pads. The nose and its contours are straight. The tip of the nose is in line with the chin, which is quite firm.

Round, largeand wide-open, the eyes are set at the right interval, thus accentuating the width of the nose even more. The color must be uniform and in accordance with that of the mantle. The most intense and most brilliant tonalities are the preferred ones.

Broad at the base, the ears are from medium to small size, rounded at their tips and with the right distance between them, so that they do not modify the round shape of the head.

Stocky and muscular, the neckline is very short, to such an extent that it seems almost non-existing.

Of semi-cobby format, the body is broad, thick, muscular and round-shaped. The bone structure is robust and the musculature powerful. The size is from medium to big.

Medium-sized, the paws are slightly less high than the length of the body. The bone structure is robust and the musculature powerful.

The feet are round and firm.

Thick at the base, the tail measures about two-thirds of the body. It has almost the same thickness, from the base to the rounded tip. In the British longhair, the tail must be abundant and plume-like.

Photo Isabelle Bonte

Shorthair : the fur is short, thick, firm and erect so much so that it opens on the neckline when the cat turns its head. It may be compared to the hair of a woollen carpet. The fur has thick down-hair and gives the impression of a good natural protection.

Longhair : the fur is semi-long, silky, with thick down-hair. The collar and the back are quite abundant.

Authorized crossings

British Shorthair x British Shorthair
British Shorthair x British Longhair
British Longhair x British Longhair

Coat

All colors are recognized

JAPANESE BOBTAIL

Photo Wikipedia

History

The Japanese Bobtail is a breed of cat native to Japan. This cat is characterized by its tail that is on itself.

In Japan, the cat is a symbol of happiness. He is associated with the lucky statuette of the greeting cat Maneki Neko (Maneki = happiness, neko = cat: the lucky cat or greeting cat), supposed to keep evils and diseases away.

When the Japanese bobtail is tricolor (tortoiseshell and white), he is known as Mi-Ke (三毛, three hairs = three colors) and is a symbol of friendship and good luck.

The Japanese bobtail has been recognized by the United States since 1968.

The Japanese bobtail comes in two varieties : shorthair and longhair.

Temper

The dominant form of Jb gene is responsible for a pompom tail. This gene is characteristic of bobtails.

He is a friendly cat and faithfully follows his owner in about all his activities. He has a distinctive voice that allows him to communicate his needs to his owners. He is a sociable cat who is unhappy when he lives alone.

Standard

Viewed in front, the head is an almost equilateral triangle, with gentle curves and high cheek bones. The nose is rather long and clearly defined by two parallel lines. Seen from the side, the forehead is slightly rounded continued by a gentle dip where the nose starts.

Relatively broad and rounded with clearly defined whisker pads. It is neither pointed nor blunt. The chin is strong.

Large, more oval than round, the eyes are wide and expressive. Viewed from the side, they are set at a rather pronounced slant. The eyeball shows a shallow curvature. All colors are accepted if in accordance with coat color. Blue or odd eyes are common in bicolor or white cats.

They are large, upright and expressive. In a front view, they are at right angles to the head. Never flaring outward, they seem to be tilted forward when the cat rests.

Neither too long nor too short, the neck is in harmony with the body.

Semi-foreign in type, the body is long, slender and elegant without being tubular. The lines are clear and finely drawn. The back is level.

In harmony with the body, the legs are high and fine, without being fragile or delicate. The hind legs are higher than the forelegs and deeply angulated. Front and back stands are parallel.

Small and oval.

The tail is naturally curved, the shape of a pompom. Carried upright when the cat is relaxed, the tail can be flexible or rigid. The hair on the tail is long enough to completely hide the bone structure.

Shorthair: the coat is soft and silky, short to medium in length with very little undercoat.

Longhair: the coat is soft and silky, medium to long with very little undercoat. It may have a ruff. The coat falls naturally and floatingly on the flanks, forming britches behind the back legs.

Authorized crossings

Japanese Bobtail shorthair X Japanese Bobtail shorthair
Japanese Bobtail shorthair X Japanese Bobtail longhair
Japanese Bobtail longhair X Japanese Bobtail longhair

Coat

Solid-colored cats should have an uniform and deep coat, from the hair root to end. Concerning bicolor and tricolor cats, called "Mi-Ke", markings should be bold and clearly visible with good contrast to give a dramatic effect.

All colors but those based on chocolate, lilac, cinnamon and fawn.

KURILIAN BOBTAIL

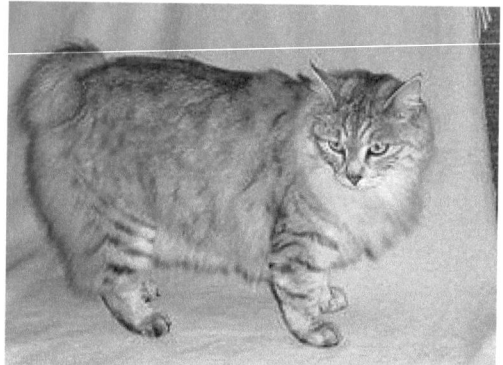

Photo Dushka

History

The Kuril Islands, located between the Kamchatka Peninsula in Russia and the northern island of Hokkaido in Japan, are known to have long been a bone of contention between Russia and Japan. There can be found a breed of cat with pompom tail, the Kurilian Bobtail.

His pompom tail is the result of a natural genetic mutation.

The Japanese bobtail may not be unrelated to the origin of the Kurilian bobtail.

The Kurilian bobtail exists in the shorthair and longhair varieties.

Temper

The Kurilian bobtail cat is curious, sociable and very intelligent

Standard

Viewed in front, the head is trapezoidal, wide at cheekbones, which are high and prominent. Viewed from the side, the forehead line is prolonged by a slight concave indentation leading to a broad straight nose.

Powerful and clearly defined, the muzzle is strong. The chin is firm.

Almost round, the eyes are large and set at a slight angle. All colors are accepted even if not in keeping with coat color.

Medium in size, the ears are set wide apart.

Powerful, the neck is rather short.

Semicobby in type, the body is compact and powerful. From shoulder blades to rump, the back is arched.

Medium long, the legs have a strong bone structure and powerful muscles.

The feet are round.

3 to 8 cm long (1.2 to 3.15 inches) without a coat, the tail is composed of one or more irregular kinks or curves.

Shorthair: short and closelying coat, with abundant guard hair and undercoat.

Longhair: semilonghair coat, with abundant guard hair and undercoat.

Authorized crossings

Kurilian Bobtail shorthair X Kurilian Bobtail shorthair
Kurilian Bobtail shorthair X Kurilian Bobtail longhair
Kurilian Bobtail longhair X Kurilian Bobtail longhair

Coat

All colors.

LAPERM

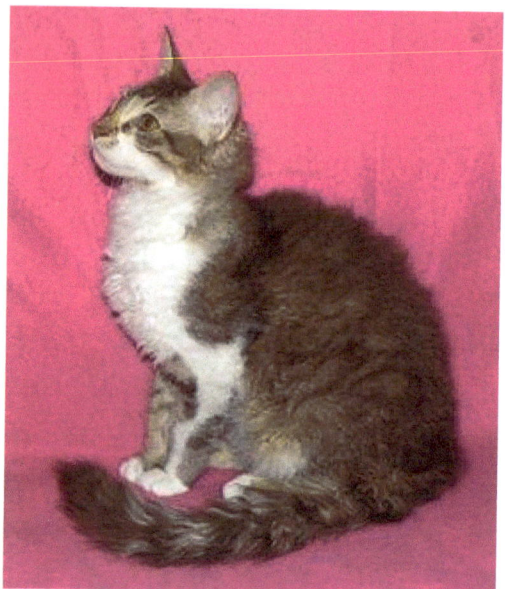

Photo Bebopscrx

History

The LaPerm is characterized by his curly hair.

He is native to the U.S. and comes from a spontaneous mutation which occurred in 1982 in the state of Oregon. By cultivating this feature, Linda Koehl created a breed.

The LaPerm exists in the shorthair and longhair varieties.

Temper

The dominant form of Lp gene gives a silky hair which is notched or wave-like. This gene is characteristic of the LaPerm.

The LaPerm is a very affectionate cat who likes to rest on the shoulder of his owners.

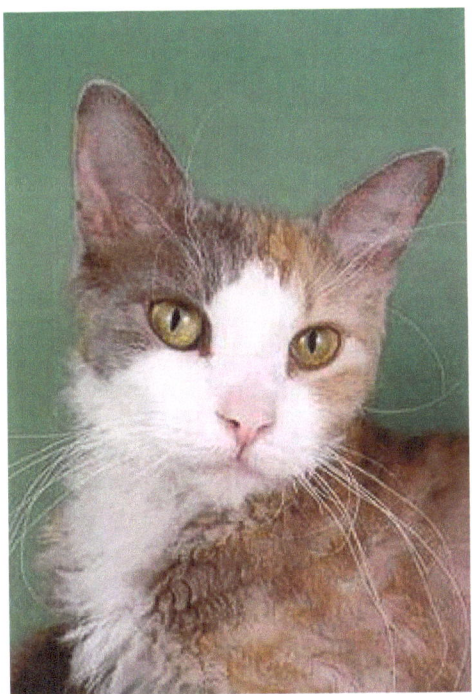

Photo Henderson30

Standard

In a front view, the head is a modified wedge with rounded contours. Viewed rom the side, the flat forehead is followed by a slight indentation between forehead and nose, without a break. The nose is broad and straight.

Rather large compared to the rest of the head, the muzzle has clearlydefined whisker pads. The chin is firm.

Medium in size, the eyes are almondshaped when the cat is quiet and round when in alert. They are slightly slanted. All colors are accepted, even if not in harmony with the coat.

Ear set follows the triangle of the head. The ears are medium-sized, but their base is wide. Lynx tips are welcome.

The neck is medium and carried erect.

Semi-foreign in type, the body is medium-long, elegant and strong-muscled.

In harmony with the body, the legs have a medium bone structure.

The feet are round.

Medium long, the tail is proportionate to the body.

The fur is curly and or wavy. The feel to the touch is unique among rex cats. Soft, it is never wiry but, on the contrary, its hair may part open when breathed upon ever so slightly.

Longhair: semi longhair. Curls are tighter on throat forming a ruff. Inside and base of ear the hair is thick and abundant with ringlets running down the sides of the head. Whiskers and eyebrows are very long and curly. The tail is plume-like.

Shorthair: medium-short and wavy fur. There are no curls on the ruff or under the ears. The tail is bushy and 'bottle-brush'like.

Authorized crossings

LaPerm shorthair X LaPerm shorthair
LaPerm shorthair X LaPerm longhair
LaPerm longhair X LaPerm longhair

Coat

All colors.

MUNCHKIN

Photo Terri Harris

History

The Munchkin is characterized by his very short legs, which sometimes earned him the nickname of basset cat. The name Munchkin comes from the Wizard of Oz legend in which Munchkins are small humanoids.

He is native to the U.S. and comes from a spontaneous mutation which occurred in 1983 in the state of Louisiana. By cultivating this feature Sandra Hochenedel created a breed. House cats and other breeds were used to fix the type as similar to the European Shorthair.

The Munchkin exists in the shorthair and longhair varieties.

Temper

The dominant form of Mk gene is responsible for the shortening of the legs. This gene is characteristic of the Munchkin. It only affects the length of the legs.

Homozygotous cats (MkMk) are not viable and usually die in utero. So, the short-legged Munchkin is heterozygotous (Mkmk) and transmits this character only to a part of his offspring.

The Munchkin cat has a kitten's character. He is very active, very sociable of a rather gregarious temperament. The size of his legs does not prevent him from running with vivacity.

Standard

The head is a modified wedge with rounded contours, proportionate to the body. Skull and forehead are very slightly rounded. The nose bridge is clearly defined, without a stop but with a gentle change of direction. The nose is more often than not straight. The head is stronger in males than in females.

Clearly defined, the muzzle is strong but without a pinch. The chin is firm.

Medium to large, the eyes are walnutshaped and set at a slight angle. All colors are accepted even if not in harmony with the coat color. It should only be as bright and luminous as possible.

Medium in size, the ears are wide at the base. They are set rather apart with a slightly rounded tip. The longhair variety has thick and abundant ear hair.
Medium in size, the neck is rather thick and strong-muscled.

Semiforeign in type, the body is medium to large and rectangular. The chest is broad, wellrounded and developed. The bone structure is strong and the musculature powerful. The shoulder blades are angulated and prominent.

Short and sturdy, the legs are wellproportioned with upper and lower forelegs equal in length and, at the back, thighs and lower legs approximately equal in length. Forelegs and back legs should be as straight as possible with medium bone structure and good musculature. Hind legs slightly longer than forelegs.

Round and firm, the feet are smaller in females than in males.

Thick at base, the tail is medium long tapering to a rounded tip. It is carried erect when the cat is in motion.

Shorthair: short, dense with lustrous appearance, the coat is closelying with medium undercoat.

Longhair: semi-long and silky, the coat has a moderate undercoat. A slight ruff is accepted. Shaggy britches and plumed tail are welcome.

Authorized crossings

Munchkin x Munchkin
Munchkin x European Shorthair

Coat

All colors.

PIXIE-BOB

Photo Nathalie Bent

History

According to legend, the pixie bob is the result of natural crossings between domestic cats and bobcats (***Lynx rufus***).

In the United States there can be found farm cats whose look is likely to give credence to this legend.

In 1985 Carol Ann Brewer, an American breeder, started a breeding program to create this race out of farm cats with this characteristic.

The breed was named Pixie-Bob and was recognized in 1994.

Genetic testing showed no traces of wild origin in the breed.

The Pixie-Bob exists in the shorthair and longhair varieties.

Temper

One of the first cats used to create the Pixie-Bob had the distinction of being polydactyl, a characteristic that is still found in this breed today.

In some countries, two polydactyl Pixie-Bobs are not allowed to mate together in order to reduce the spread of the gene inside the breed. A polydactyl Pixie-Bob can be mated with a non-polydactyl Pixie-Bob.

The Pixie bob is a very much balanced cat, affectionate and docile. He likes to follow his master around like a dog.

In some countries, polydactyl cats are not allowed to compete at shows.

Standard

The medium to large head is the shape of a large inverted pear when seen in frontal view. Seen from the side, the forehead is slightly rounded and continued by a gentle stop. The nose is wide, slightly convex, with a gentle bump. Nose leather is brickred and particularly large.

Large and strong, the sharply defined muzzle has fleshy whisker pads. The chin is well-developed and covered with a coarse fuzzy fur. It is firm and in a line with the tip of the nose.

Medium in size, the eyes are the shape of a softened right-angled triangle. The bushy brows form a first horizontal line going down the nose in a vertical line. The triangle is stopped by a diagonal line from the inner corner of the eye to the ear. Set wide apart, the eyes are slightly covered by heavy eye lids, giving the impression that the cat is half asleep. The make-up consists of a cream or cream-white band around the eye and Mascara lines from the outer corner of the eye down to the cheeks. Preferred colors range from gold to hazel. Gooseberry green is allowed.

Mediumsized, the ears are large at base with a rounded tip. They are set as much on top of the head as on the side, slightly tilted outward. Lynx tips are desirable as well as pale thumb prints on the back of the ears.

Medium in size, the neck is strongmuscled.

Long and strongly built, the body is medium to large. The shoulder blades are prominent, giving a rolling gait. The flanks are deep and powerful. The chest is broad and well-developed. The back is not level: there is a downward slope behind the shoulders, continued by a slight upward slope to the prominent hind legs that are slightly higher than the shoulders. The rump gently slopes downward to the tail. A belly pouch is desirable in males as well as in females.

Short, the tail is preferably flexible but kinks and curls are accepted. Minimum length: 2 inches (approximately a thumb's length). Maximum length: down to hock when the leg is extended. Tail length is determined by the last bone part that can be felt. When at rest, the tail is carried low.

The legs are long and muscular with a strong bone structure.

Large and broad, the feet are almost round with big phalanxes and fleshy toes.

Shorthair: soft coat, woolly and resilient to the touch. The coat, which is not too close to the body, is longer on the belly.

Longhair: the very soft coat is closer to the body than in the shorthair variety. It does not exceed 5 cm (2") In both short- and longhair varieties, the hair on the head and face is very fuzzy, with thick brows and a downward growth. The fur breaks open easily and seems well-suited to hard climatic conditions. Seasonal changes may be noticed in the texture, coat color and hair length. In summer, the coat is shorter than in winter and the spotted pattern is clearly visible. In winter, the coat gets denser, emphasizing the ticking and giving the impression that the coat is sparkled with frost.

The only color accepted in championships is a brown spotted tabby well lightened by an important ticking. Spots are randomly scattered on the body (broken mackerel or blotched patterns). Rosettes are accepted and the belly is spotted. All shades of brown spotted tabby are accepted, even if warm shades are desirable.

The wild look of the coat color is given by a mousegrey base color with an inverted ticking: darker bands are close to the skin and lighter color bands at the end of the hair. Color of agouti bands ranges from brown to dark brown, each hair displaying several alternate bands. The light bands at the end of each hair give the impression - more obvious in winter - that the coat is sparkled with frost.

The belly is not ticked and tends towards cream-white, still on a mouse-grey base. The chin and throat are paler. Paw pads, back of legs and tail tip are dark brown or black.

Authorized crossings

Pixie Bob X Pixie Bob

Coat

Black, spotted tabby pattern only (brown spotted tabby).

SELKIRK

Photo Ciaccia

History

The Selkirk Rex is characterized by his curly hair.

He is native to the U.S. and comes from a spontaneous mutation which occurred in 1987 in Wyoming. Jeri Newman, a breeder of Persian, cultivated this feature using Persians, Himalayans, American Shorthairs, British Shorthairs. The cat's name came from a mountain in Wyoming.

The breed was recognized in 1992.

The Selkirk with normal hair is known as the Selkirk Straight. He doesn't have access to any championship.

The Selkirk Rex and the Selkirk Straight exist in the shorthair and longhair varieties.

Temper

The dominant form of gene Se makes the hair curly and abundant. This gene is characteristic of the Selkirk Rex.

The temperament of the Selkirk Rex is a combination of those of breeds that are at his origin. He has the cuddly temper of the Persian, the playfulness of the Exotic Shorthair, the reserve and relaxation of the British Shorthair.

Photo Jean Goyer

Standard

The head is broad with wellrounded contours whichever way you look at it. Cheeks are full. The top of the head is rounded, prolonged by a slightly concave curve. The nose is short and broad. A slight stop is allowed. Adult males have well-defined jowls.

When viewed from the front or from the side, the muzzle is set in a well-defined circle with firm and full whisker pads. The nose and edge of nose are straight. The end of the nose is in line with the very firm chin.

Round, big and wide-open, the eyes are set well apart which strengthens the breadth of the nose. The eye color should be uniform and in relation to coat color. The more intense and brilliant tones are preferred.

Wide at the base, the ears are medium to small, with rounded tips. They are set well apart, they should fit into the rounded outline of the head.

Stocky andmuscular, the neck is very short, almost non-existent.

Semi-cobby in type, the body is big, thick, strong-muscled and round. It shows a strong bone structure and powerful musculature. It is medium to large in size.

Medium in length, the legs are slightly shorter than length of body. Their bone structure is solid and they are strongly muscled. The feet are round and firm.

Wide at base, the tail's length is about two thirds of body length. It is almost the same width from the base to the end, which is round.

The Selkirk Rex's coat is dense and plushy, forming more or less loose individual curls. The mutation affects each type of hair (guard, down and awn) and guard hair tend to have a coarse texture. Curliness should be more obvious on the neck, throat, belly and tail. The whiskers and eyebrows are curly.

Shorthair: medium in length, the coat is dense, soft and plushy. It should not be too close-lying.

Longhair: semi-long, the fur is dense, soft and very curly. The curls, longer than in Shorthair, give the impression of being loose and individual.

Authorized crossings

Selkirk X Selkirk
Selkirk X British Shorthair
Selkirk X British Longhair
In all Selkirk varieties (short hair or long hair; Rex or Straight).

Coat

All colors.

TONKINESE

Photo Jessica Hubert

History

Crossings between Siamese and Burmese were observed from the nineteenth century onwards. It was in 1930 that Canadians were interested in this type of crossing and they called Golden Siamese the breed they got.

The resulting race was renamed Tonkinese in 1960 and recognized in 1974.

Changing tastes led to the search of a more elongated morphology in the Siamese, so Burmese X Siamese marriage gradually gave place to the marriage of Tonkinese with Tonkinese, although the contribution of the Siamese and Burmese is allowed.

The Tonkinese exists in the shorthair and longhair varieties.

The longhaired Tonkinese is sometimes called Tibetan.

Temper

The Tonkinese combines features of Siamese and Burmese.

Less exclusive than the Siamese, he is attached to his owner and does not like solitude. He is a playful active cat needing physical exercise.

Photo Wikiarea655

Standard

Just slightly longer than wide, the head is a modified wedge with gently curved contours. The side lines of the triangle formed by the jaw hinges are clearly defined and slightly rounded. Viewed from the side, the top of head and forehead are slightly rounded and prolonged by a gentle stop at the base of the nose, with a slight rise from stop to tip of nose.

The muzzle is mediumlong, gently prolonging the lines of the wedge, neither pointed nor excessively rounded. The chin is firm.

Placed as much on the side of the head as on the top, the ears are medium in size, wide at base with rounded tips. They are covered with very short hair and leather may show through.

Walnutshaped, the eyes are slightly slanted. Eye color: aqua (blue-green) in minks, sky blue to violet in colorpoints, gold to green in sepias, brilliant, deep and clear colors preferred.

Medium long, the neck is strong-muscled, especially in males.

Semi-foreign in type, the body is medium, strongly muscled though not stocky. The chest is broad and gently rounded.

Fairly slim, the legs are in the right proportion to the body.

More oval than round, the feet are medium.

Medium long, the tail tapers to a slightly blunted tip.

Shorthair: particularly soft to the touch, the coat is short, dense, silky and closelying.

Longhair: semilong and fine, the coat is silky and closelying. There is almost no undercoat. The coat is shorter on the shoulders and gets longer on the flanks. Britches and tail are bushy. There may be a ruff.

Authorized crossings

Tonkinois X Tonkinois
Tonkinois X Siamois except particolor
Tonkinois X Balinais except particolor
Tonkinois X English Burmese
Tonkinois X Tiffany, only sepia, not tipped

Coat

In the Tonkinese, Siamese C_s gene (colorpoint) is codominant with Burmese C_b gene (sepia), neither gene canceling or modifying the other, but giving an intermediate color (mink).

Sepia Tonkinese

Sepia pattern ($C_b C_b$). This specific pattern lightens body color in a gradual shading of delicate warm hues, leaving back and extremities (ears, muzzle, legs and tail), which are called "points", slightly darker than the flanks, throat and underside.

Mink Tonkinese

Mink pattern ($c_b\ c_s$). c_s gene (colorpoint) is codominant with c_b gene (Sepia), neither of them nullifying or modifying the other, but giving an intermediate color. Contrast is less marked than in colorpoint cats.

Point Tonkinese

Colorpoint pattern ($c_s\ c_s$). This pattern noticeably lightens body color, the points being much darker. Because of the polygenes, the coat may be darker than Siameses' and eye color may display a less intense shade of blue.

D – BREEDS EXCLUSIVELY WITH SHORT HAIR

AMERICAN SHORTHAIR
AMERICAN WIREHAIR
BENGAL
BOMBAY
AMERICAN BURMESE
CALIFORNIA SPANGLED
CEYLON
CHARTREUX
CHAUSIE
DEVON REX
DONSKOY
EUROPEAN SHORTHAIR
GERMAN REX
HAVANA BROWN
KORAT
OCICAT
PETERBALD
RAGDOLL
SAVANNAH
SINGAPURA
SNOWSHOE
SOKOKE
SPHYNX
THAI

AMERICAN SHORTHAIR

Photo dustin Warington

History

After the Egypt of the pharaohs and Europe, the saga of the domestic cat brought him on to settlers' ships sailing off to conquer the New World. Once there, his ancestral qualities as protector of crops made him a very popular farm cat.

In the twentieth century, advances in the fight against rats gradually deprived him of his utility role and turned him definitely into a pet.

With the rise of the breed cat, and the search for standard, enhanced beauty and sometimes originality, many domestic cat breeds have at last been recognized as such. In the United States people realized how precious this cat was and so it was raised to the rank of breed cat under the name American Shorthair.

Temper

The American Shorthair is a medium sized cat with an athletic body and a short, glossy fur, who has kept the authentic aspect of his ancestors, American farm cats, harvest protectors and mouse hunters. Balance is essential in this rustic cat Any morphological exaggeration that would disturb his physical potential is to be rejected.

He is affectionate, emotional and moderately active but not aggressive. Patient with children, he accepts the presence of a dog.

Standard

Medium in size compared to the body, the head, viewed in front, is squarish. His full cheeks give him a sweet open expression. The nose is medium short with the same width all along. Viewed from the side, the skull is rounded, with a slight stop preceding the nose.

Typical of the breed, the muzzle, without being extremely short, is clearly defined and square. The jaw is firm and strong. The chin is strong.

Medium to large, the eyes are rounded and set at a slight angle. The color, bright and luminous, should be uniform.

Medium in size, the ears are not too widely open at the base. Slightly rounded at tip, they are set wide apart.

An important element in the overall balance of the cat, the neck is medium in length and muscular.

Semi-cobby in type, the body is rectangular in shape and strongly built. The chest is broad and the slightly rounded shoulders and hindquarters have the same width. The back is level and broad. Strong bone framework.

The legs have a sturdy bone structure and a powerful musculature. They are straight and medium long.

The feet are round, with good paw pads.

Medium long, the tail is thicker at base and tapers slightly to a rounded tip.

Short and even, the coat is dense and lustrous.

Authorized crossings
American Shorthair X American Shorthair
American Shorthair X American Wirehair

Coat
All colors but those based on chocolate, lilac, cinnamon and fawn

AMERICAN WIREHAIR

Photo Heikki Siltala

History

The American Wirehair is a breed of cat native to the United States. This cat is characterized by its curly haired coat.

The American Wirehair is consecutive to a distinctive genetic feature which appeared in the American Shorthair in 1966.

The breed was recognized in 1987.

Temper

The dominant form of gene Wh makes the hair very curly and hard to the touch. This is the gene that characterizes the American Wirehair.

The American Wirehair is affectionate, emotional and moderately active but not aggressive. Patient with children, he accepts the presence of a dog.

Standard

Medium in size compared to the body, the head, when viewed in front, is squarish. His full cheeks give him a sweet open expression. The nose is medium short with the same width all along. Viewed from the side, the skull is rounded, with a slight stop preceding the nose.

Typical of the breed, the muzzle, without being extremely short, is clearly defined and square. The jaw is firm and strong. The chin is strong.

Medium to large, the eyes are rounded and set at a slight angle. The color, bright and luminous, should be uniform.

Medium in size, the ears are not too widely open at the base. Slightly rounded at the tip, they are set wide apart.

An important element in the overall balance of the cat, the neck is medium in length and muscular.

Semi-cobby in type, the body is rectangular in shape and strongly built. The chest is broad and the slightly rounded shoulders and hindquarters have the same width. The back is level and broad. Strong framework.

The legs have a sturdy bone structure and powerful musculature. They are straight and medium long.

The feet are round, with good paw pads.

Medium long, the tail is thicker at base and tapers slightly to a rounded tip.

The American Wirehair was named after its very specific coat, which is like steel wool. Its fur is made of crimped, spiked, bent and hooked hair. The combination of all those types of hair gives a unique touch to the coat, which is springy, dense and coarse. The overall springy appearance is of more importance than the crimping of each hair. The quality of an American Wirehair's coat can be properly judged when stroked and not by examining each hair. The ear hair and whiskers are curly. The fur should not show any crimping that would make it look like a Rex cat coat.

Authorized crossings
American Wirehair X American Wirehair
American Shorthair X American Wirehair

Coat
All colors but those based on chocolate, lilac, cinnamon and fawn.

BENGAL

Photo Namibi bengal

History

As early as the end of the nineteenth century, at the first feline shows, cats were exhibited as crossings between domestic cats the wildcats.

During the first part of the twentieth century, some observations about crossings between domestic cats and wildcats were published and relevant experiments took place.

During the sixties, several leopard cats or Bengal cats (***Felis bengalensis***) were imported into the USA, particularly as domestic animals, and there too, experimental crossings were made. It was during those years that some clubs came into existence, aiming at promoting the hybridization of the domestic cat with the wild cat. The term "Bengal" then began to be used to describe these cats.

During those years, pharmacological researchers used hybridization between the leopard cat and the domestic cat for immunology research against feline leukemia.

One of the scientists having taken part in these experiments, Jean Sugden (later Jean Mill), thought, during the seventies, of taking advantage of the interest these hybrids might create, to fight against the utilization of feline furs in the clothing industry. In 1980, she was able to collect her first four leopard cats from a laboratory which had used them in the context of its immunology research. In this way, she began her hybridization works.

The male specimens born of hybridization are sterile for several generations. It is therefore necessary to utilize domestic male cats for the first few generations. Being a breeder of the Egyptian Mau, her choice naturally turned towards this cat whose spotted pattern might allow the pattern of the leopard cat to be preserved.

One of her trips brought her to the zoo of New Delhi. There, just in front of the cage of the leopard cats, was the enclosure of the rhinos. And with them lived two tabby cats with copper colors which had been pointed out to her by her friend, the director of the zoo. These cats, Toby and Tasha of New Delhi, were taken to the USA, recognized as Egyptian Maus and utilized in the program of creation of the Bengal and also in a program of enrichment of the color of the bronze Egyptian Mau. The first generations that came up were at times declared as Maus and at other times as Bengals. The great adventure of the Bengal had finally started. The breed was recognized as experimental in 1983. In addition to the Egyptian Mau, other breeds of domestic cats were used to create the Bengal, particularly the Burmese, the Siamese, the Abyssinian and the domestic cat.

In 1987, the uncertain course of genetics research gave life to a Bengal with a marble pattern. The unexpected success caused this pattern to be admitted among the standards.

During the eighties, other hybridization experiments took place, particularly the crossing of the domestic cat with the Margay (*Felis wiedii*) under the name of Bristol cat. The last Bristol cats were inserted into the

Bengal breed in 1991 with the aim to widen their genetic patrimony. Incidentally, this contribution helped obtain rosettes in the pattern.

The Bengal has been the victim of a fashion phenomenon, which has led to an important production by breeders of different competence. Some of them consider the Bengal breed as moderately stabilized, both in terms of morphology and character. However, quality breeders produce cats in conformity with the standard of the breed, which are of great beauty and pleasing character.

The intensive utilization of the Egyptian Mau to create a breed has at times led to cats whose appearance reminded one very much of the Egyptian Mau. Such cats are still met with in breeding farms where quality production is not the main concern. The good quality Bengal, in conformity to its standard, does not look like the Egyptian Mau any more.

Photo Seduisant

Temper

Specimens born of the hybridization of a wild cat and a domestic cat are called F1. The specimens of the following generation are called F2. And so on.

In hybridization, males are sterile for several generations (4 to 6), which accounts for the utilization of domestic cats as male reproducers to create a new line. Generations F1 to F3 are considered as wild, banned from shows and subject to specific measures concerning their possession..

Depending on the lines, F4 to F6 Bengals cannot be totally stabilized as regards morphology or character.

The specimens too close to their wild ancestors can prove timid and, at times, even scary. This trait disappears when the number of generations separating them from their ancestors is sufficiently high.

The Bengal is lively, intelligent, curious, sportive, talkative and very affectionate, especially with other animals and with kids. It loves water and particularly appreciates to perch itself high up

Photo Gabel Le Bonne

Standard

The head, with rounded contours, is the shape of a triangle, longer than wide. It is rather small compared to the body, but without exaggeration. The expression of the Bengal's head must be as far away as possible from that of a domestic cat. The curve of the forehead, slightly rounded, gently meets the stop of the nose, without any interruption, and continues in a line practically straight to slightly convex up to the end of the nose. The cheeks are high and marked. The nose is wide with a typically bulging skin. For males, jowls are authorized.

The muzzle is formed by very developed whiskers which generate a slight pinch. Seen in profile, the strong chin is in line with the tip of the nose.

Big, set wide apart, the eyes are oval, almost round but never globular. The eyes are green, gold, blue or aquamarine, depending on the color of the mantle. The deepest and most brilliant tonality is the most appreciated.

Of medium to small size, the ears are rather short, with a wide base and a rounded extremity. They are spaced out the length of one ear. In profile, they point forwards. "Lynx tips" are unwanted.

The neck is long, muscular and well attached. Body: long, it is strong-muscled, and has a robust bone framework. This gives the Bengal the look of a powerful but graceful cat.

The legs, of medium length, strong and muscular, have a robust bone framework.

Big and round, the feet of Bengals have prominent toes.

Medium to short, the tail is thick at the base, getting hardly thinner and ending in a rounded extremity.

The fur is short, thick, well distributed all over the body and exceptionally sweet and silky to the touch. The fur can be somewhat gold-sprinkled, an effect called "glitter", this tonality, however, must not constitute an advantage over a cat devoid of "glitter".

Spotted pattern and rosettes: two types of dots are admitted, rosettes and spots, which are set at random or aligned horizontally. The rosettes are composed of at least two different colors and can have the shape of a printed paw, or of an arrowhead or of a ring. They are preferred to the simple spots but are not requisites. Whether spots or rosettes, the contrast with the background color must be extreme, with distinct forms and rims. The shoulders are mottled all over, whilst the legs and tail are spotted or ringed. The belly must imperatively be spotted. On the head, the typical make-up of the tabby cats is strongly marked. The whiskers, the throat, the bottom of the hair on the belly, and the inside of the paws are whitish, the lightest white possible. Both spotted patterns and rosettes compete in the same class.

The marble pattern differs from the tabby blotched one. Here, the classical marks (oyster shell, butterfly wing) are elongated horizontally so much so that they resemble marble veins or the marks of the clouded leopard. The bands of the base color must be as broad as the veins; they also are closer to each other at the centre. Preference must be given to the mantles presenting at least three tones: the base color, the color of the marks and the intense color underlining these marks. The contrast must be extreme. The belly must imperatively have drawings. On the head, the typical make-up of the tabby cats is strongly marked. The whiskers, the throat, the base of the hair on the belly and the inside of the paws are whitish, as pale as possioble.

Coat

Patterns: spotted, rosettes, marble.
Colors: black (brown, silver, smoke), blue.

AMERICAN BURMESE & BOMBAY

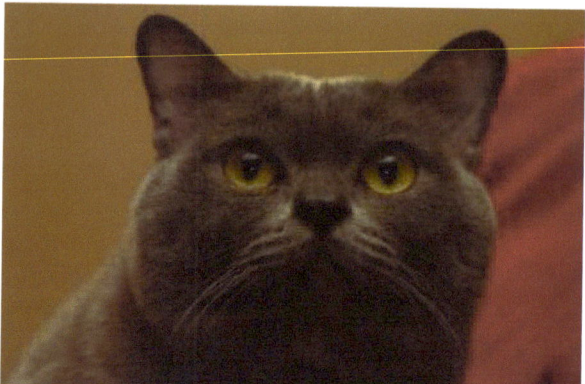

Photo Bjtripp2

History

Burmese means Burman in English. In spite of this, this breed has nothing to do with the Birman which nowadays is called Sacred Cat of Burma in order to avoid such confusion. The first Burmese descend from Wong Mau, a she-cat carried to the USA in 1930 by Joseph Thompson, a medical officer. This cat should have resulted from the crossing of golden-eyed Siamese and dark colored cats. Crossed with dark colored Siamese, she made it possible to get cats with a unique color, sepia. This new breed was immediately recognized in the USA.

This origin accounts for a rather strong resemblance between the Burmese and Siamese of that time, the main difference being the color with gene c_s of the Siamese (pattern colorpoint – only the extremities are colored) being replaced by gene c_b of the Burmese (pattern sepia – attenuation of the color on the whole body but the extremities).

With the evolution of tastes, breeders have caused the morphology of the cats to evolve. The Siamese has become much more long-limbed, the traditional Siamese being renamed Thai. As for the Burmese, it has evolved on the one hand towards the Burmese called American (a cat of cobby format), on the other hand towards the Burmese called British (a cat of semi-foreign format). Nowadays these two cats have sufficiently different morphologies to be considered as different breeds.

In 1958 Nikki Horner, an American woman from Louisville, wanted to create a breed that resembled a miniature black panther. To do this, she married an American Burmese and an American Shorthair and made numerous other crossings to get what she wanted. The result was a beautiful black cat with golden eyes, which was called Bombay.

Photo Pititebilette

Temper

The Burmese is a stable and loving cat (sometimes called "cat-dog"), energetic, playful and extremely endearing. He is very outgoing and has a strong personality.

He is said to gossip with a softer voice than the Siamese.

Photo Bjtripp2

Standard

Medium in size, the head is rounded, with no flat plane whichever way you look at it. The profile is all curves with a rounded forehead and a visible stop. The nose is slightly hooked and bulging.

Round and short, the muzzle is broad. The chin is firm and round, without off bite.

Large and set wide apart, the eyes are round. Eye color ranges from copper to gold for the Bombay copper being preferred. From gold to yellow for the American Burmese, gold being preferred.

Mediumsized, wide at base and slightly rounded at tip, the ears are set wide apart and slightly tilted forward. A slight bald area between the upper eye lid and the inner ear is accepted.

Medium to short, the neck is well developed.

Cobby in type, the body is compact with a broad rib cage and is surprisingly heavy for its size. Shoulders and hips are slightly rounded. Bone framework and musculature are sturdy.

Medium in size, the legs are in the right proportion to the body.

Rounded, the feet are medium in size.

Medium, never short or whip-like, the tail tapers to a blunt tip.

Short, fine, the coat is close-lying and satin-like.

Authorized crossings

Bombay X Bombay
Bombay X American Burmese (seal sepia only)
American Burmese X American Burmese

Coat

The Bombay's coat is jet black to the root.

In the adult American Burmese, coat color gets more intense at the extremities of legs, tail, mask and ears, which are darker. Exception should be made for kittens and younger cats concerning coat color and texture.

American Burmese

Sepia pattern and Seal sepia colors, blue sepia, chocolate sepia, lilac sepia.

Bombay

Black

CALIFORNIA SPANGLED

Photo Flamingice007sg

History

The Californian Spangled is a breed of cat native to the United States. This breed, characterized by its spotted tabby coat evoking the leopard, was created by screenwriter Paul Casey who wanted this cat to look like a small leopard.

Attempts at creation of this breed began in 1970. Abyssinian, Siamese, British, American Shorthairs and alley cats from Asia and Egypt were used. In 1986, after 11 generations, the breed was finally launched.

With the rise and success of Bengal, the Californian Spangled has virtually disappeared.

Temper

The California Spangled is a bright, energetic, curious and very affectionate cat.

He is a cat with an athletic, long, strong and cylindrical body. His coat is short and sweet, except on the tail and under the belly where the hair is longer. Spots cover the back and sides, fine lines extend from the top of the skull to the shoulders.

Standard

Medium in size, the head is wedge shaped, with high prominent cheek bones. The skull is slightly rounded. There is a small stop between forehead and nose.

Strong and well developed, the muzzle displays clearly defined whisker pads. The chin is firm and thick.

Medium to large sized, the eyes are almond shaped. Wide open, they are set obliquely, which is emphasized by the high cheek bones.

Medium large, the ears are relatively short with a wide base and rounded tips.

The neck is medium, strong-muscled and tubular.

Semi-foreign in type, the body is long, slender and muscular. It may seem heavier than it really is.

Medium long, the legs are strong-muscled with strong bones.

Large and round, the feet have prominent toes.

The tail is of medium length and equally thick from base to tip.

Short and closelying on the face, neck, back and flanks, the coat can be slightly longer on tail and abdomen.

<u>Coat</u>

All colors. spotted tabby pattern only.

CEYLON

Photo Wikipedia

History

Ceylon is a breed of cat from Sri Lanka discovered by Dr. Paolo Pellegatta in 1984.

This medium sized cat is characterized by his shorthair coat with a ticking pattern. However, other tabby patterns are also allowed.

Ceylon has been recognized since 1993.

Temper

Ceylon is a sociable and confident cat.

The pattern of Ceylon is due to T_a gene, which is responsible for the ticking pattern.

The ticking pattern is responsible for the characteristic color of the Abyssinian. In the late nineteenth century, when the recognition of breeds and the organization of cat shows began, an Abyssinian cat was simply a ticketed cat. The remainder of the Abyssinian standard was developed gradually. Scientific studies have shown that the ticking pattern was typical of the Far Eastern origin of this breed.

For ticketed tabby cats, one can identify the "chaus" pattern (no tabby markings) and the "Bentota" pattern (with tabby markings on head, legs and tail). Each of these patterns competes separately.

Standard

Medium in size, the head is a modified wedge. Viewed in front, the skull is slightly rounded and the cheek bones are clearly defined. Viewed from the side, the forehead is flat and continued by a concave line at the base of the nose, not a stop. The nose is short.

Slightly rounded, the muzzle gently finishes the triangle of the head. The chin is not very firm.

The upper line of the eyes is straight slightly sloping down toward the nose. The bottom line is rounded. The eyes are rather large, their color ranges from green to gold.

Medium to large, the ears are wide at base with rounded tips. They are set high on the skull, and rather close. Lynx tips and a lighter colored thumb print marking at the back of the ear are desirable.

The neck is rather long and graceful, with the head coming well off the shoulders.

Semicobby in type and medium long, the body is compact. The abdomen is rounded. The body displays a powerful musculature and a rather fine bone structure.

Medium long, the legs have a rather fine bone structure. Hind legs are higher than forelegs.

The feet are round.

Short, fine and silky, the coat has hardly any undercoat. Ticking (light and dark bands alternating on each hair shaft) is more obvious on chest, back and flanks.

Coat

All colors but those based on chocolate, lilac, cinnamon and fawn.
Tabby pattern only.

CHARTREUX

Photo Isabelle Bonte

History

The Chartreux, also called cat of the Carthusians, is a breed of short-hair cats native to France.

It is said that it came from Turkey or Iran and reached the west at the time of the crusades.

The Chartreux gets its name from the legend that it lived in the monasteries of the Carthusian monks where it hunted rats .Those were the times when the bubonic plague was devastating Europe. The feline is said to have then shared the monks' vow of silence. That is why even now this cat mews very little.

It was utilized by furriers, due to its thick rather woolly fur.

It was accurately described by Buffon in the XVIIIth century.

Photo Isabelle Bonte

Temper

The Chartreux is a robust cat with entirely blue short hair and copper or orange eyes. It's a solid cat whose chubby cheeks make its face look so round as to give the impression that it's going to smile.

It is esteemed for its hunting abilities and its uncommon intelligence. It is flexible and agile and its behavior evidences the qualities which have permitted this cat to survive even difficult times and conditions.

The Chartreux has inherited the independent character of the true felines. It is playful, sociable and joyous; it has a cat-dog temper and adores to follow its master from one room to another.

It represents the French feline breed *par excellence*. It was the cat of Joachim du Bellay, who wrote a wonderful poem in memory of his own cat, Belaud. It was also the companion of Charles de Gaulle and of Colette.

Standard

Trapezoid, with the lower base bigger than the upper one, the head is broad with rounded contours. The cheeks are full and well developed, especially in males more than 2 years old. The profile is slightly concave at the level of the eyes with a high flat forehead between the ears. The nose is straight, wide and moderately long.

Even if not pointed, the muzzle is fairly narrow, if compared with the whole of the head, and has developed whisker pads. The chin is firm.

Big and expressive, the eyes are wide open with their external corners slightly raised and moderately spaced. Their color ranges from yellow to orange.

Narrow at the base, slightly rounded and of medium size, the ears are placed high on the head.

Strong, thick and short, the neckline is muscular.

Of semi-cobby format, the body is robust with broad shoulders and a deep chest. It has a medium length with a strong bone structure and a thick powerful musculature. The females are remarkably lighter, even if they retain a robust look.

Of medium length, the paws have a strong bone framework and a powerful musculature, particularly weldeveloped in males.

The broad feet are slightly oval.

Of average length, the tail is thick at the base and then gets pointed further on. It is soft, fairly short, with a thick fur, rather woolly and raised, seemingly almost waterproof. Downhair is abundant.

Coat

All blue-grey tones, from pale blue-grey to pronounced blue-grey, are accepted, provided they are uniform from the root of each single hair up to its extremity.

The truffle is slate-grey, lips and pads are blue.

Ghost tabby marks are tolerated in kittens less than one year old .

CHAUSIE

Photo Pschemp

History

The Chausie is a breed of cat native to the USA. This cat is characterized by its structure which relates it to the Chaus (**Felis chaus**).

The Chausie is the result of hybridization between a Chaus and a tamed cat.

The first crossings took place by the end of the sixties in order to obtain a savage type cat close to the Chaus, but with the character of a tamed animal. Abyssinians, Orientals, Bengals and also feral cats having a savage look were chosen.

The breed is recognized as a new one. It cannot enter a competition.

Temper

The cats born of the hybridization of a feral cat and a tamed one are called F1. The subjects of the following generation are called F2 and so on.

In hybridization, males are sterile for several generations (4 to 6), hence the utilization of tamed cats as male reproducers in order to create a new line.

Generations F1 to F3 are considered as savage, banned from shows and subject to specific dispositions concerning their possession.

Depending on the lines, subjects F4 to F6 cannot be totally stabilized in terms of morphology or temperament.

The Chausie is a big cat which moves like a feline. Active, it bears solitude with difficulty and needs companionship.

Standard

A big sweet triangle when seen from the front, the head has a medium size. The cheek-bones are marked and angular. The front is slightly cambered. Seen from the side, this soft curve changes slightly direction at the beginning of the nose and forms a slight concave slope. The very broad nose is slightly hooked and the truffle bulging.

The muzzle is in harmony with the remainder of the head with rounded whisker pads. The chin is firm.

Of medium size, the eyes, which form a slightly flattened oval, are slightlyat a slant. Gold to yellow is the preferred color, hazel or green is accepted.

High and big, the ears stand close to each other. Broad at the base, they have a rounded tip. Tufts are desirable, but cats without them must not be penalized. A thumb print of pale color back of the ear is sought for.

Strong- muscled, the neckline is of medium size and width.

Long and powerful, the body is rectangular. The musculature is powerful but flat and the chest broad and deep; the thorax must not be round-shaped.

Medium long, the paws are strong-muscled with a medium bone frame. The rear ones, particularly powerful, evidence this cat's aptitude to run and jump.

Round, the feet are small if compared to the size of the cat.

Rather thick, the tail measures about ¾ of the length of the tail of a normal cat, with a reduced number of vertebrae. A longer tail is accepted. In any case, it must be well articulated.

Short to medium and close to the body, the fur must however have a sufficient length to allow each hair to have at least four alternate bands, pale and dark, called ticking. The down-hair participates in the specificity of themantle, silky and elastic in some specimens.

Authorized crossings

Chausie x Chausie
Chausie x Abyssinian
Chausie x tamed cat not belonging to any breed
Chausie x Felis Chaus

Coat

Black, pattern ticked tabby.

DEVON REX

Photo Bebopscrx

History

The Devon Rex is a cat breed native to England. It is characterized by its curly-haired coat.

It is the result of a genetic mutation discovered in 1960, in Devonshire.

The Devon Rex was recognized in 1979

Temper

The recessive form of Re gene causes the three types of hair to be short in length. The fact is they are wavy. This gene is characteristic of the Devon Rex.

The Devon Rex is well-known for being a playful, mischievous sort of cat and a bit of a rascal, too. It is an acrobatic cat hating being left alone and needing the presence of other cats. It is very close to humans and requires much attention. It also delights in following its master around and taking part in all the activities of the family.

Photo Pathfinder Linden

Standard

Rather small if compared to the body, the head, seen from the front, evidences three convex arcs formed by the lobe of the ears, the prominent cheek-bones and the muzzle.

Seen from the side, the flat skull is prolonged by a convex forehead continued by a net stop at the level of the nose. This break is situated between the eyes.

Short and well developed, the muzzle is delimited by an important pinch. The whisker pads are prominent. The chin is strong and well developed.

A very particular attentionis paid to the proper occlusion of the jaws.

Big and wide open, the eyes are oval. All colors are accepted, if in accordance with the mantle.

Remarkably big and very low placed, the ears are so wide at the base that the lobe of the ears marks a stall. Rounded at their extremity, with or without "lynx tips" (tufts), they are covered by a fine fur. The temples are often bare.

Thin and muscular, the neckline causes the head to stand out from the shoulders.

Of semi-cobby format, the body is nice, firm and strong-muscled. The chest is wide and very open.

Long and high, the paws have a rather thin bone frame, if compared to the body, with, in any case, a powerful musculature.

The feet are oval and small.

Long and thin, the tail is covered by a short curled fur.

Thin and soft, the fur is short with a thick irregular curling.

The thickness of the fur varies with the different parts of the body, the upper regions (face, ears, back, sides, upper part of the paws and tail) are more furnished with hair than the lower ones (throat, chest, abdomen and inner side of the paws).

The fur covering the skull and the neck is often so short that it cannot be serrated.

Fully bare areas are considered a minor fault in the kitten, but a serious one in the adult.

The whiskers, rather rare, are short and curled.

Coat

Colors: all

DONSKOY

Photo ooznu

History

The Donskoy, also called the Don Sphynx, is a breed of cats native to Russia. This cat is characterized by the absence of hair.

On numerous occasions, hairless cats appeared spontaneously as a result of natural genetic mutations. It was one of these naturally mutating cats that was discovered in 1987 in Rostov on Don, and then bred in order to create the Donskoy.

The breed was fixed by using European, Persian and Siberian cats.

Temper

The dominant form of the gene, (Hp gene), is also responsible for the almost complete absence of the three types of hair. This gene is characteristic of Donskoy and Peterbald.

The curly whiskers are distinctive features in newborns.

The "brach" variety has curly hair often hard on the body with parts that may be bare.

The Donskoy is an active, affectionate, intelligent and very sociable cat.

Photo ooznu

Standard

Wedgeshaped with high cheek bones, the head has wrinkles on the forehead, somewhat fewer above the eyes. The profile is almost straight, with a medium long nose.

Short and rounded, the muzzle is slightly pinched. Curly whiskers may be absent. Jaws and chin are shallow.

Slightly almondshaped, the eyes are slanted. Eye color should be in accordance with coat color.

Large, set high on the head, the ears are slightly tilted forward. The end of the ear is rounded, continuing the vertical line of the sides of the head.

Semi-foreign in type, the body is sturdy, well built, muscular yet elegant. The chest is broad and the abdomen rounded with extra skin at groin. Broad croup.

Long and muscular, the legs are well-proportioned to the body.

Oval, the feet have clearly defined toes.

The tail is long and whip-like.

The skin is elastic, with wrinkles on the head and neck, underside, groin and belly.
There can be short sparse fur on the muzzle, ears, feet, tip of tail and genitals.

Coat

All colors are admitted.

Tabby cats, whether they are mackerel, spotted or blotched, are judged together with the other cats since the pattern is not always visible on the skin.

EUROPEAN SHORTHAIR

Photo Didier Hallépée

History

Leaving the Nile, the domestic cat (**Felis silvestris catus**), a descendant of the African Wildcat (**Felis silvestris lybica**), followed the trade routes travelled by the caravans, went on board vessels and travelled along with the Roman legions going back to Rome. From there, it gradually spread across Europe and much later to the New World.

Protector of harvests in Egypt, it became a hunter of rats and other noxious animals on the old continent, assuming in this way a modest role against the propagation and spread of the black plague. A utility animal for a long time, it lived mostly in the vicinity of man rather than with him. Its reputation as a diabolical animal and its role as an intimate of witches sometimes earned it many disappointments.

In Europe, the cat has kept the genetic diversity of its origins and has, on the one hand, enriched it while adapting to the extreme conditions of some countries, and on the other, has interbred, at times, with its cousin, the European Wildcat (**Felis silvestris silvestris**).

It became a pet starting from the sixteenth century onwards. By the twentieth century, progress in the struggle against rats in cities and then in rural areas, gradually put an end to its utilitarian role and turned it into a pleasure animal even though there are still some populations of this cat breed roaming free in our built-up areas.

During the nineteenth and twentieth centuries, there was the growth of the purebred specimens, and research for establishing the standard, improving the beauty and at times the originality of this breed.

By the end of the twentieth century, finally, people realized what a treasure their house cat was. In spite of an ample variety of colors and a very rich genetic pool, it has a rather homogeneous morphology, which has led to its being raised to the rank of breed cat. As such, it has been designated as European cat, and, later on, as European Shorthair.

Little things differentiate our traditional domestic cat from the European bred cat: it is conformity to a standard and the existence of a filiation certified by a pedigree which cause the difference.

In other parts of the world, the domestic cat has had a slightly different evolution and acquired slightly different local characteristics. There too, this treasure of a cat, shaped over time, has been finally recognized and thus it was that the British shorthair, the American shorthair or the Arabian mau came into existence.

Photo Lance94

Temper

The European cat is robust, agile, rustic and playful, able to adapt easily to new situations.

From its feline past, it has kept its artful, curious, valiant character and, , its occasional inclination to steal.

The kittens are frail at birth and need very much attention and care from their mother during their first month and its constant presence for about three months. This accounts for the docile and affectionate nature of this feline and its, looking for company and for cuddles.

From its feline origins and its past as an alley cat, it has kept great qualities as a hunter, an instinctive mistrust and a taste for independence and liberty. A very good explorer, it does not hesitate in going to see what's going on a little far away and gradually widens its territory. But it is also a home-staying cat, very much attached to its quarters or its house where it always comes back... unless it gets lost.

Having been bred in a family, and manipulated lovingly from its youngest age by its human family this cat is a company animal particularly affectionate and attached to its owners. If grown up without any human contact in its infancy and submitted to the vicissitudes of an alley cat, its instinctive mistrust will gain the upper hand and it will avoid all human contact even if displaying a strange attraction for this funny two-legged animal: however, it will be tamed and will finally appreciate the vicinity of man and the comfort of its environment. It will deign to be petted without, however, permitting anyone to manipulate it.

The European Shorthair is a cat of breed with a filiation duly certified by a pedigree, grown in a family and with close contact with humans since its birth. So, it has kept the best features of its feline origins together with all the qualities expected from a companion with which we humans will share a good part of our lives.

Photo Fleshgrinder

Standard

Longer than wide, the head is rather round with weldeveloped jaws. The front and the skull are slightly rounded. The base of the nose is sharply defined, without a stop but with a slight change of direction. The nose is straight, of medium length and of the same width all along. Clearly defined, the muzzle is strong, but without a pinch. The chin is firm.

From medium to large in size, the eyes are rounded and slightly aslant. The color, from orange to yellow and to green, must be as brilliant, luminous and uniform as possible.

Medium sized, the ears are as high as wide at their base. They are set rather wide apart from one another and have a slightly rounded tip. Muscular and soft, the neck is of medium size.

Of semi-foreign type, the body is of medium to big size and rectangular. The chest is wide and well developed.

The bone framework is strong and the musculature powerful.

Sexual dimorphism is pronounced.

The legs are of medium length, strong and solid. Round feet.

Thick at its base, the tail is of medium length and gets thinner and thinner ending in a rounded tip.

Short, thick and glossy, the fur is close-lying all over the body without undercoat in excess.

Coat

All patterns but colorpoint.

All colors but those based on chocolate brown, lilac, cinnamon and fawn.

GERMAN REX

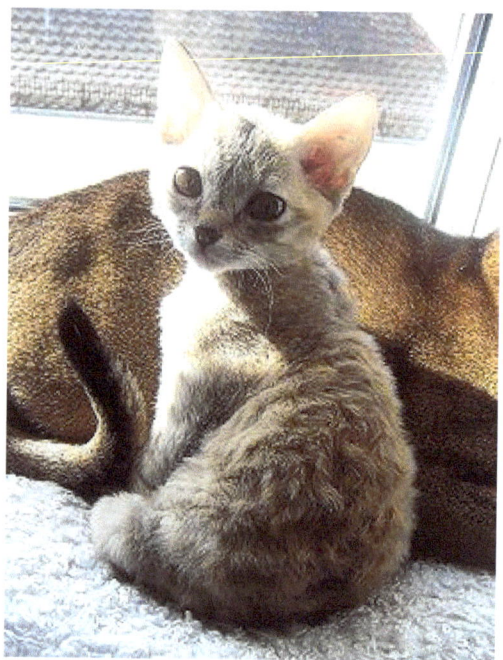

Photo Gerver

History

The German Rex is a breed of cat native to East Prussia (a part of Russia since 1945) characterized by its shorthaired, wavy and very soft coat.

The first subjects were discovered in Konigsberg (Kaliningrad) in the early 30s by Erna Schneider.

Other subjects were discovered in 1951 by Dr. Rose Scheuer-Karpin.

The German Rex has been used in Cornish Rex programs against skin problems.

Some cat associations accept the German Rex. Others identify it with the Cornish Rex.

Temper

The particular aspect of the German Rex fur is due to the recessive form of a gene responsible for the absence of guard hair. This cat's guard hair is short and wavy. The whiskers are short and curly.

The gene responsible for this feature is different from the one of the Cornish Rex. Indeed, in the latter it is awn hair that is missing.

The German Rex is an active, affectionate and patient cat.

Standard

Longer than wide, the head is rather round with well-developed cheeks. Skull and forehead are slightly rounded. The nose base is clearly-defined, without a stop, but with a slight change of direction. The nose is straight, medium in length and has the same width from base to end.

Well-defined, the muzzle is strong, without a pinch. The chin is firm.

Medium to large, the eyes are rounded and set slightly obliquely. The color, ranging from copper to gold or green, should be as brilliant, bright and uniform as possible.

Medium in size, large at the base, the ears have rounded tips. The back of ear should be covered with fine yet dense hair, the inside only slightly furnished with hair.

Muscular and supple, the neck is medium-sized.

Semi-foreign in type, the body is medium to large and rectangular. The chest is broad and well-developed. The body has strong bones and a powerful musculature. Difference in size between males and females is important.

Strong and firm, the legs are medium in length.

The feet are round.

The tail is medium in length, thick at base and tapering to a rounded tip, with abundant coat.

Short, plush and velvety , the German Rex's coat displays waves like the Cornish Rex's, except that the lack of guard hair, and not dawn hair like in the Cornish, gives a thicker coat structure than the latter's. However, thickness can vary according to subjects. The whiskers are short and crinkled.

Authorized crossings

German Rex X German Rex
German Rex X European Shorthair

Coat

All colors but those based on chocolate, lilac, cinnamon and fawn

HAVANA BROWN

Photo Dave Scelfo

History

The Havana Brown, also known as the Swiss Mountain cat or Chestnut Oriental Shorthair, is a breed of cat native to Britain. This cat is characterized by its short hair coat the color of chocolate.

Chocolate-colored cats existed in the ancient kingdom of Siam. They were credited with the power to ward off evil spirits.

In 1950 Baroness Von Ullmann crossed a chocolate point Siamese with a black European to get a chocolate brown cat. The breed was recognized in 1958 under the name Chestnut Brown then Havana Brown – Havana because their color is reminiscent of Havana cigars.

Temper

The Havana Brown is a curious, lively, playful cat, enjoying the comfort of his home. He likes to "talk" with his favorite human.

Standard

Longer than wide, the head is well proportioned to the body. Seen from the side, the forehead is flat and prolonged by a definite stop at eye level. Jowls are allowed in males.

Typical of the breed, the muzzle is so square that it seems to be an added element. The whisker pads are clearly defined, and the chin is firm and strong.

Oval, the eyes are large, wide open but not protruding. The only permitted color is any vivid shade of green, provided it is uniform.

Large and round tipped, the ears are set wide apart. Viewed from the side, they are slightly tilted forward, which gives the cat a very alert look. They are very slightly furnished with hair.

Medium long, the neck is l strong-muscled.

Semi-foreign in type, the rectangular body is firmly muscled.

Long, if compared to the size of the cat, the legs are elegant with a strong bone structure.

The feet are oval.

Medium in length, the tail is slender, narrow at base and tapers to a fine tip.

Short, soft and silky, the coat is sometimes slightly thicker on flanks. The deeper the color, the better, as uniform as possible, without white hairs or tabby markings.

Coat

Colors : chocolate, lilac.

KORAT

Photo Heikki Siltala

History

The Korat is a cat whose breed comes from Thailand. This small cat is characterized by its short-haired coat with silvery blue ends and green eyes.

This breed has been known to the kingdom of Siam since the fourteenth century as the si-Sawat. Korat cats belonged to the category of lucky cats. His name si-Sawat means "the color of Sawat" because his color is reminiscent of the look of Sawat seeds, seeds with protective virtues. The word "Sawat" means happiness or, luck and refers also to a soft silky material.

The si-Sawat combined all these qualities. His is a natural breed originating in the Khorat plateau (hence his name), north-east of Thailand, whose breeding was reserved to noble families. His export was strictly prohibited.

With reference to the tree that gave him his name, the male was called Maledi (seed). The female was known as Doklao, named after the gray flower of the wild lemon-grass.

The si-Sawat was very popular at the royal court of Siam. In 1894, King Rama V gave a few Siamese cats to the General Consul of the United Kingdom, letting him believe that this cat was the emblem of Siam, in order to preserve the exclusivity of precious lucky Korat for his kingdom. From this comes the legend of the Siamese. Thus, the West, fascinated by the Siamese, forgot for many years to take any interest in natural cat breeds from Asia.

The Korat was discovered by westerners in 1896 and recognized as a breed in 1966.

Korat breeders insist that the genealogy of their cats goes back to original subjects from Thailand.

Temper

The character of the Korat is similar to that of his cousin, the Siamese. He is extremely loyal and shows a strong attachment to his owner. He is a very communicative cat that has a wide range of mews at his command.

The Korat is calm and shows a great interest in game throughout his whole life. His intelligence enables him to quickly learn a few little tricks.

Standard

The head is heart-shaped, with curved lines. Viewed in front, the prominent brow ridges form the upper curve of the heart, whereas the muzzle is the bottom part of it. Seen from the side, the forehead is large and flat, continued by a slight stop at nose level. The end of the nose is curved downward like a lion's.

Neither square nor pointed, the muzzle completes the triangular shape of the heart. The jaws are strong and the chin is firm.

Oversized, when compared to the face, the eyes are rounded when open but keep an oriental slant when half-closed. Set wide apart, they are luminously green. Kittens under 2 years may have amber-yellow eyes.

Large, with rounded tips, the ears are set high on the head with a wide open base. The outside is covered with a fine textured fur and the inside is sparsely furnished with hair.

Medium in size, the neck is strong-muscled.

Semi-cobby in type, the body shows smooth curved lines with a broad chest and rounded hips. The rump is round. The Korat is powerful and extremely muscular, yet never heavy.

Mediumsized, the legs are proportioned to the body so that height at shoulders is identical to the distance from base of neck to base of tail. Bone structure is medium but with strong musculature.

The feet are oval.

Medium long, the tail is thick at base and tapers to a blunt tip.

Medium short, the coat is simple and closelying, glossy and satiny. The coat is blue, each hair being silver tipped, enlightens the fur with a silver sheen effect, even more intense where the coat is shorter. The coat on the spine is apt to break as the cat moves.

Coat

Blue

OCICAT

Photo Tom Bjornstad

History

The Ocicat is a breed of cat native to the United States. This medium cat is characterized by his tawny spotted coat reminiscent of the ocelot.

In 1964 an American breeder, Mrs Virginia Daly, who wanted a few additional tabby point Siamese made crossings between Siamese and Abyssinian and obtained a kitten with an original coat looking very much like an ocelot.

Other breeders crossed Siamese, Oriental, Abyssinian, Egyptian Mau and American Shorthair to get a cat looking like the ocelot.

The race was called Ocicat (ocelot cat) and was recognized in 1986.

Temper

The Ocicat is a loving cat, very active and sociable with humans and other animals. He cannot stand loneliness , so the term "cat-dog", is often used to describe him. He is said to be as affectionate as the Siamese but not as expressive.

Standard

The head is a modified wedge, with rounded contours and clearly defined cheekbones. Seen from the side, there is a slight curve between the gently rounded forehead and the nose, without any break.

Broad and clearly defined, the muzzle is rather square in a frontal view, and rather long when seen from the side. The pinch between the cheekbones and the muzzle should not be too important. The jaws are firm, showing proper bite. The chin is strong.

Oval, the eyes are large, set wide apart and slightly slanted. All eye colors, except blue, are accepted even without any relationship with coat color, but eye color should be as uniform as possible.

Medium in size, the ears are set as much on top of the head as on the side. Lynx tips are desirable.

The neck is arched.

Semi-foreign in type, the body is rather long, sturdy and deep but without being heavy. The chest is broad and the ribcage slightly rounded. The back is level or slightly higher at the hindquarters. The musculature is powerful and elegant, giving an athletic appearance. Even if large cats are preferred, balance and harmony are more important than size. Females are noticeably smaller than males.

Medium long and strong-muscled, the legs have firm bones .

The feet are oval and compact.

Medium to long, the tail is rather thick at base and tapers slightly down to the tip.

Fine, tight, silky and close-lying, the coat is long enough to carry several bands of ticking. When those bands of color meet, they form clear markings contrasting with the lighter ground color. Hair forming the spots is lightcolored with dark tips. All hair shafts are ticked except at the tip of the tail. Ground color should be light enough for a distinct contrast with darker markings, even in dilute colored coats. Chin, throat, inside of legs and underside are lighter than the back.

All markings should be clearly visible, whatever the angle at which one looks at the cat. Markings on the face, legs and tail should be darker than those on the body. The forehead displays the characteristic M of tabbies and the eyes the typical Mascara lines. A second line beyond the make-up gets paler close to the ears. Clear straight lines start from the M on the skull and become elongated spots on the spine. The markings are longer on the shoulders and make a transition between the lines and the spots. The rest of the body is covered with irregularly-shaped spots that are never aligned thus departing from the mackerel tabby markings. The broken blotched pattern, with a spot circled by other spots on the flanks, is appreciated. There are several broken necklaces at the throat and spots on the belly. The legs display large bracelets that may be broken and of different sizes. The tail has rings down to its dark tip.

<u>Coat</u>

Colors: black, blue, chocolate, lilac, cinnamon, fawn
Spotted tabby pattern only

PETERBALD

Photo Peterbald

History

The Peterbald is a breed of cat native to Russia. This cat is characterized by his hairless coat and his oriental appearance.

This breed was created in St. Petersburg in 1994 by crossing a Donskoy with an Oriental in order to create a hairless Oriental.

The breed was recognized in 1996

Temper

The dominant form of the Hp gene is responsible for the almost complete absence of the three types of hair. This gene is characteristic of Donskoy and Peterbald.

There are 4 varieties:
- naked cats;
- cats with very short hair, called "velvet";
- wirehaired cats, known as "brush";
- cats with normal hair.

The Peterbald is described as a temperate, peaceful, energetic and curious cat.

From the Siamese and the Oriental, he has inherited his capacity for exclusive attachment.

Photo Irina Polunina

Standard

Viewed in front, the head is medium, long and triangular. The top of the head and the forehead are flat or slightly rounded. 3 types of profiles are accepted: perfectly straight, slightly convex or in 2 lines: the line of the forehead continuing the line of the nose without a break. Cheeks are flat. Jowls are accepted in adult males.

When facing the cat, the nose is inside the triangle of the head, without a pinch. The end of the nose should not be narrow. Viewed in profile, the nose is long and straight.

The jaws are medium in size. The chin is firm, in line with the end of the nose.

Mediumsized, the eyes are oriental. Almond shaped and wide apart, they are set with a slant toward the nose, in harmony with the triangle of the head. Color of the eyes is the deepest vivid blue for pointed cats, and the deepest vivid green for traditional cats. Odd eyes (green and blue) are accepted in parti-colored cats. Odd eyes and blue eyes are accepted in white Peterbalds.

Large, wide at base, set wide apart, the ears continue the triangle of the head.

Long, slender and elegant, the neck sets off head and shoulders.

Oriental in type, medium in size, the body is long, tubular and firm. It appears strikingly dense when handled. It is athletic and slender with a firm lithe musculature. Equal width at shoulders and hips. Fine bone structure.

The tail is in harmony with the length of the body and of legs.

Long and elegant, the legs are in harmony with body length. Their bone structure is fine and their musculature firm.

The feet are oval and small.

Bald variety: the skin is elastic and totally bald, with a rubber-like feel. The whiskers are often missing.

"Velours" variety: the skin is covered with a very short coat, with a touch ranging from chamois to short-napped velvet. The extremities often display longer hair. The whiskers are curled or broken.

"Brush" variety: the coat is short, curly and coarse, sometimes sparse on the body. The whiskers are curled and broken.

In "bald" and "velours" varieties, the cats can have wrinkles on the head, neck, forelegs, underside, groin, and belly. Type should be the priority. If equal in type, the "velours" variety with the shortest possible hair (chamois touch) should be preferred.

Neither fat nor thin, the cats of this breed group are slender, not skinny.

Authorized crossings

Peterbald X Peterbald
Peterbald X Siamois
Peterbald X Oriental

Coat

All colors

RAGDOLL

Photo Simone Johnsson

History

The Ragdoll is a breed of cats native to the United States. This breed was created in 1963 by Jane Baker, in California. This cat has the particularity of relaxing completely when carried about, like a ragdoll.

The breed was recognized in 1963.

Temper

When carried, the Ragdoll becomes as loose as a ragdoll.

This trait is inherited from its earliest infancy: when the mother carries the kittens, she normally does so to change location, to bring the kittens closer to a source of food or take them to a place deemed to be good for their learning process. This type of shifting may be dangerous for the kittens; this is why nature has endowed them with the instinct of relaxing while their mother is carrying them around.

This instinct diminishes with age, but never disappears completely. So, a simple manner of controlling a cat is to hold carry it by the skin of its neck.

In the Ragdoll, when it is carried, this relaxation remains as complete as it was during its first days of life.

Standard

Shaped like an equilateral triangle, the head has a rounded outline. Seen from the front, the space between the ears seems to be flat. Seen in profile, the skull and forehead are rounded and prolonged y a slight cavity at the level of the nose, which is straight (a profile defined as "toboggan"). Of medium length, the muzzle is weldeveloped and rounded; the chin is strong.

Quite big and oval, the eyes are slightly slanted even if they are not oriental. The color is the most intense blue possible.

Of medium size and situated on the extension of the triangle of the head, the ears are broad at the base. The tips are rounded. Seen from the side, they are slightly tilted forward. The neckline is short and strong-muscled.

Long and powerful, the body is rectangular with a broad round chest. The width between the shoulders is equal to that between the hips. In spite of being heavy, the Ragdoll is not fat; only a belly pocket is accepted.

Of medium size, proportionately to the rectangle formed by the body, the paws have a strong bone structure and a powerful musculature. Round and strong, the feet do have an inter-digital pilosity.

Long, the tail ideally reaches the base of the scapulae. Broad at the base, it is very dense, ending in a tuft.

Semi-long and silky, the fur is formed by an important covering of guard hair and of little down-hair. A ruff starting from the back of the ears and prolonging itself on the neck is appreciated. The fur is short and dense on the fore-paws, longer on the back ones, where it can even form knickerbockers.

Coat

Colorpoint pattern
Points: the ears, the mask, the feet and the tail have the base color of the cat, darker than the body and homogeneous, if possible. Body: its color ranges from egg-shell to milk-white, depending on the base color of the cat. The chest, the ruff and the chin can be somewhat paler. Slight shades on the body are allowed.

Mitted pattern
Points: the ears, the mask, the paws – the feet excepted – and the tail do have the base color of the cat, darker than the body and homogeneous if possible. A white blaze on the nose and/or between the eyes, whether interrupted or not, is accepted provided it does not reach the truffle. The chin must be white. Forefeet: white gloves, regular and firm. Back paws: wholly white up to the middle of the thighs. The white color must cover the hocks. There must not be colored patches in the white. Body: its color goes from egg-shell to milky-white depending on the base color of the cat. The chin must be white and extend in a white band of variable width, to the ruff and the chest, running between the forepaws and under the belly up to the beginning of the tail.

Bicolor pattern
Points: the ears, the mask and the tail have the color base of the cat, darker than the body and homogeneous if possible. The mask has a white inverted V which must also be symmetrical and not extend beyond the external edges of the eyes. The truffle is pink. Body: its color varies from egg-shell to milky-white depending on the base color of the cat. The chest, the belly, the paws and the feet are white. A few white patches are accepted on the back and sides.

Van pattern
Points: their color is limited to ears, the upper part of the mask and the tail. The truffle is pink. Body: white, but a few small egg-shell to milky-white patches, provided they do not add up to more than 20% of the surface of the body, head and tail included.

SAVANNAH

Photo Jason Douglas

History

The late twentieth century was marked by the desire of some American breeders to produce homegrown mini-Panthers, domestic wild-looking cats. This was to be achieved by crossing domestic cats with small wild felines.

After the Bristol cat created out of the Margay (Felis weidii), the Bengal created out of the Asian Leopard (**Felis bengalensis**) and the Chausie created out of the Chaus (**Felis Chaus**), here is the Savannah created out of the Serval (**Leptailurus serval**, previously **Felis serval**).

Some people think that hybridization of wild races is a wonderful contribution to the domestic cat. Others consider it's no good. Anyway, these practices have brought about new breeds like the Savannah.

The Savannah is a new breed of cat native to the United States. This large cat results from a crossing between a Serval and a domestic cat: a Bengal, which he is very close to. He has many physical similarities with the Serval: the size, the color and the characteristic ear shape.

The first Savannah was created in 1986 by Judee Frank. Together with Joyce Sroufe, she set a standard. The breed was recognized in 2002.

Temper

The cats born of the hybridization of a wild cat and a domestic cat are called F1. The cats of the next generation are called F2. And so on.

In hybridization, the males are sterile for several generations (4-6), hence the use of domestic cats as breeding males to create a new line.

F1 to F3 generations are considered wild, banned from shows and subject to specific dispositions concerning ownership.

Depending on lines, F4 through F6 subjects cannot be fully stabilized as regards morphology or character.

The exceptionally friendly temper of the Serval, makes it possible to have pleasant cats rapidly. However, as the wildness of ancestry is never faraway, you should be ready to face the unpredictable reactions of a wild feline.

The Savannah is a large cat, very intelligent, curious, sociable, active, gentle and affectionate. He jumps higher and runs faster than any other domestic cats. He loves to go into water.

The desired characteristics are those of the Serval: small head, big ears set high, very long body, long legs, relatively short tail and spotted coat.

Standard

Small in proportion to the body, the head, viewed in front, is a triangle that excludes the ears. The skull should be very slightly rounded. The forehead, flat to slightly convex, is prolonged by a very small indentation at nose bridge. The nose, broad and straight, ends in a rounded tip.

The muzzle lines are clearly defined, without a pinch. The chin, though not receding, is not well-marked.

Medium in size, the eyes are almond-shaped. Set wide apart, they should ideally display characteristic white tear-like markings (in agouti cats only). Eye color, from gold to green, is not related to coat color. Intensity alone is to be taken into account.

Large and set high on the head – the inside base being almost set at the top of the skull – the ears are wide at base with rounded tips. The typical thumb print of agouti cats is desirable on the back of the ear (in agouti cats only).

Long and strong-muscled, the neck is lean and elegant. The head is straight and held with grace.

Semi-foreign in type, the body is characterized by a very deep rib cage and a slightly higher rump. The hips and thighs are long, fully muscled and a bit oversized.

The legs are long and slender, yet strong. Viewed from the back, the hind legs are very high.

The feet are small and oval, with elongated toes.

Rather thick, the tail is around ¾ of a normal cat tail. It does not reach the ground when the cat is standing. Flexible and very expressive, it displays rings in agouti cats, with a black colored blunt end.

Short to medium, the coat has a very special feel to it: rather coarse guard hair cover a dense somewhat silkier undercoat, with notably softer textured spots. Whatever the color, all Savannahs should display the same spotted tabby pattern with, on top of it, as many small spots as possible on legs and face. The spots are always black, and can be round, oval or elongated. The underside is spotted.

In brown spotted tabby Savannahs, ground color ranges from gold to orange, without ticking. Throat and belly should be off-white. Ground color is silver in silver cats. In black and black smoke subjects (nonagouti cats), the ghost tabby markings should be clearly visible. The Savannah's nose leather is brickred with a black outline, or solid black. It is solid black in black or black smoke subjects.

Authorized crossings

Savannah X Savannah
Savannah X Egyptian Mau
Savannah X Oriental Shorthair
Savannah X Ocicat
Savannah X Serval

Coat

Black, tabby and smoke pattern only.

SINGAPURA

Photo Squeezeveasel

History

According to legend, the Singapura is a natural adaptation of domestic cats to the: living conditions prevailing on the roads of Singapore (city of the lion).

Their small size is supposed to come from their habitat, the sewers of Singapore, whose conduits are small and narrow.

The first three specimens were carried over from Singapore by Tommy and Hal Meadow in 1975. In 1981, another lover brought in a specimen from Singapore, too, which was included into the breeding program.

It would seem, however, that these first three cats, which happened to be small, resulted from crossings between Abyssinians and Burmese and accompanied Tommy and Hal Meadow in 1974 on their stay in Singapore, before reaching the USA with them.

The utilization of the Burmese is proved by genetic studies.

But, as the movie "The man who shot Liberty Valance" says: "When legend is more beautiful than reality, print the legend".

The Singapura was recognized as a breed in 1982, and, following this recognition, the Singapore Tourist and Promotion Board (STPB) adopted the Singapura as a touristic mascot under the name "kucinta" (from the Malaysian "kucing" = cat, and "cinta" = love).

The exports of Singapore cats are at present under strict control.

Temper

The Singapura is active, curious and playful. Affectionate, it seeks human contact.

The Singapura is the smallest of domestic cats.

Standard

Rounded and quite small, the head has, seen from the front, a rounded skull prolonged by high broad cheek-bones.

Seen in profile, the forehead is slightly bulged and continued by a hollow slope at the beginning of the nose. This one, rather short, is slightly bulged. Of medium length, the muzzle is broad and delimited by a clearly defined pinch. It must be neither sharp nor narrow. The chin is firm and well developed.

Big and very expressive, the eyes are wide open and nut-shaped. Even if spaced out by at least the width of one eye, they must be neither rounded nor protuberant. Green in all its nuances is the preferred color, provided they are uniform. The blue color is not accepted.

Big, attentive and moderately sharp, the ears are cup-shaped with a bell-shaped base. This open base is mostly responsible for the general impression of largeness of the ears. They are set apart the width of one ear. The inside of the ears is very hairy.

The short neckline is thick. Of semi-cobby format, it has a compact body with a wide-open rounded thorax.

The paws, strong and thick at their beginning, get ever thinner and end up in a rather thin bone-frame.

The feet are small, oval and firm.

Ideally, long enough to reach the scapulae, the tail, slightly dense at the base, gets ever thinner and ends up in a rounded tip.

Fine, silky and without down-hair, the fur is close-lying. Short, it must anyway have a sufficient length so that each hair can have several bands, alternately pale and dark, called ticking. It is longer on the spine. Kittens may have a longer and woollier fur than adults.

Coat

The bottom of the hair is the color of old ivory. The ticking, the makeup marks, the pads, and the extremity of the tail are dark brown or black. The truffle, brickcolored, is delimited by a dark brown or black edge.

The pattern is genetically ticked tabby sepia, that is, each hair has an alternation of at least four ivory, dark brown or black bands, but the whisker pads, the throat, the chest, the belly, the inner side of the paws and the lower side of the tail are not speckled.

The ticking is more evident on the backbone and on the tail. The base of the hair is always pale and the extremity dark. The foreside of the forelimbs and the knees must ideally have tabby marks. The head has the patterns typical of tabby cats: inverted M on the forehead, slight makeup marks around the eyes and on the cheeks.

SNOWSHOE

Photo Wikipedia

History

The Snowshoe is a breed of cat native to the United States. He looks like a Siamese cat (old type) with white feet.

In the 1960s, a breeder of Philadelphia wanted a Siamese with white-gloved paws. The Snowshoe is the result of his breeding program based on Siamese, American Shorthair and Birman.

Meanwhile, the Siamese has evolved, that is why we now describe the Snowshoe as a Thai with white feet.

The Snowshow exists in two patterns: bi-color (white is distributed all over the body) and gloves (only legs and part of the head are white).

Temper

The Snowshoe is a faithful cat devoted to his owner, but less exclusive than the Siamese. He is lively, intelligent and full of temper.

Standard

The shape of the head is a modified wedge, equilateral in shape, with rounded contours. The area between the ears seems flat, when facing the head. The cheekbones are set high and the bone structure should be visible, even in adult males that have more developed cheeks. Viewed in profile, the forehead is straight and continued by a slight curve on the nose. The latter, medium in breadth, is straight more often than not. A small bump is accepted.

Medium in length, the muzzle is rounded with a slight pinch. Strong chin.

Rather large, the eyes are oval to round. They are slightly slanted without being oriental. All shades of blue are allowed.

Medium-sized, continuing the line of the wedge, they are large at base with rounded tips.

Medium in size, the neck is strong and muscular.

The body is semiforeign in shape, harmonious and strong muscled. Dense, it appears less heavy than it truly is. Females are smaller and lighter than males.

Rather long, the legs are relatively fineboned and have weldeveloped muscles.

Oval, the feet are in proportion to the body.

Medium in length, the tail is thicker at base and tapers slightly to the end.

Short to moderately short, the coat is soft and silky. Dense, it is not closelying.

Coat

2 patterns are allowed: bicolor and mitted. The distribution of white in the mitted pattern is one of the most difficult to obtain as it is very precise and rather unpredictable. Only the four feet should be white and the face should show an inverted V.

Mitted

Points: ears, mask, legs – except feet – and tail show the basic point color of cat, darker than body and as uniform as possible.
Front feet: white and even mittens.
Back legs: white to midthigh. There should not be white-colored spots
Body: color from eggshell to milky-white according to color of points. Darker shades are allowed on shoulders and hips. Throat, chest and stomach are white, but proportion of white should not exceed one fourth of coat color.

Bicolor

Points: ears, mask, feet and tail show basic point color of cat, darker than body and as uniform as possible. Mask shows an inverted V that should be as symmetrical as possible and not extend beyond outer edge of eyes. Nose leather is pink.
Body: color from eggshell to milky-white according to color of points. Darker shades are allowed on shoulders and hips. Chest, stomach, legs and feet are white. A few white spots are allowed on back and flanks, proportion of white not to exceed half of total surface of coat.
Colored spots on paw pads are accepted in both mitted and bicolor cats.

SOKOKE

Photo Wikipedia

History

Attracted by the human habitat where he found so many good things to hunt and eat, the African wildcat (***Felis sylvestris lybica***) managed to domesticate man in ancient Egypt and then to conquer Europe and the New World.

In the heart of Africa, in Kenya, lives the Khadzonzos (which means "like bark" in the dialect of Giriama). This cat with a mottled shimmering coat lives next to tribes just like the cat that used to live by the side of Egyptians on the Nile. This coexistence seems to have been there for several centuries.

Is he a direct descendant of the African wildcat, the descendant of Egyptian cats who followed the trade routes to the wilds of Africa, or the descendant of cats that came with colonization? Nobody knows and DNA tests have not identified any genes of wild felines.

The Khazonzos was discovered in 1978 by Jeni Slater, introduced into Denmark by Gloria Moeldrop and bred as the Sokoke (the name of the Arabuko-Sokoke forest from which it originates).

The Sokoke was recognized in 1993.

Temper

The Sokoke cat is a lively, playful cat. He loves climbing and swimming, he is both pretty independent and sociable.

Standard

The head is a modified wedge, small in size if compared to the body. The top of the skull is almost flat, the cheekbones are high and clearly defined. The profile shows a very soft indentation at the base of the nose, which is medium in length and straight.

Clearly-defined, the muzzle is not pinched, with a firm chin.

Almond-shaped, the eyes are large, set wide apart and slightly oblique. Their color is amber to green.

Mediumsized, the ears are wide at base with rounded tips. Lynx tips are desirable.

The neck is slender and muscular, the shoulders clearly setting off the head..

Semi-foreign in type, the body is medium long, slender and muscular. The chest is round and well-developed.

High and long, the legs have a sturdy bone structure. The angularity of the hind legs is pronounced, which is characteristic of the breed.

The feet are oval.

Medium to long, the tail is thicker at base and tapers to the tip.

The coat is very short, closelying and glossy, with no undercoat. Marble pattern looks like a classic tabby slightly elongated and blurred by ticked hairs in the solid areas (black markings), both of them being hallmarks of the Sokoke breed.

Coat

Only in black, classic pattern (Brown tabby)

SPHYNX

Photo Schuminweb

History

If hairless cats have always existed, the Sphynx, with its odd way of walking, appeared as a feline breed by the end of the seventies in Canada. Brought from Toronto to Holland by Dr. Hernandez, the first Sphynxes originated a line in France before reaching the USA. The nudity of the Sphynx, which varies from a perfectly hairless skin to a "velvety" down, is caused by a spontaneous mutation. The particularity of this breed is not limited to the skin alone, as it is also recognizable by its uncommon typology.

Photo Schuminweb

Standard

Medium-sized, rounded and well developed, the muzzle is delimited by an important demarcation which emphasizes it against the skull. The upper lips are clearly rounded. The chin is firm and sharply defined.

Lemon-shaped, the eyes are big, wide-open and expressive. All colors are accepted if in harmony with the coat.

Very big and set low , the ears, at their base, are wide. They must appear disproportionate to the head. They are rounded at the extremity.

Medium-sized, the neck is strong-muscled. It is arcuated and sharply sets off the head from the shoulders.

Of semi-cobby size, the body is firm. The musculature, clearly visible under the skin, is rounded. The chest, barrel-shaped, is wide and deep. The abdomen is very round, looking as if the cat had just been eating; this particular feature does not imply, however, that the cat is obese.

The hips and the rump are rounded.

The legs are fairly fineboned, but have firm and clearly outlined muscles. The forelegs are slightly bent.

Oval, the feet have long thin toes, with well modeled phalanxes. The pads are thicker than in the other feline breeds, and this gives the impression that the Sphynx walks on something like airbags.

Whip-like, the tail is long and slightly thick at the base and looks like a rat tail.

The skin of a Sphynx can vary from total nakedness to a "velvety skin". The skin of kittens is very much wrinkled..

Adults must keep as many wrinkles as possible, especially on the head, without this affecting in any way the cat's normal functions.

The whiskers and eyebrows are scarce or missing.

<u>Coat</u>

Categories: all
Divisions: solid, tabby, silver/smoke, solid and white, tabby and white, silver/smoke and white
Colors: all
The color of the coat matches the missing fur

THAÏ

Photo Trinny True

History

Since long, the Siamese has seduced cat lovers both by its unique beauty due to its colorpoint pattern (which it has transmitted to other breeds), and by its unique character which makes it a very attaching and exclusive companion.

The Siamese of the early century had a wellrounded face like that of our European cat, as can be seen in the Walt Disney animated cartoon, Lady and the Tramp.

Since then, Siam has become Thailand, but for us the Siamese keeps alive the memories of that time.

With the evolution of tastes, breeders turned it into a cat more and more long-limbed, in order to enhance its oriental look.

But several nostalgic people have remained attached to the traditional Siamese and have wanted to keep its so captivating face intact.

This old type Siamese ended up being raised to the rank of a breed cat under the name of Thaï in homage to its original land , Siam, which later was to become Thailand.

Temper

The Thaï, nicknamed "our grandma's cat", the ancestor of our modern Siamese, has retained its so captivating characteristic features: strong personality, exclusive attachment to its master, marked dominance over the rest of the feline race. It is lively and talkative.

Standard

Slightly longer than broad, the head, as seen from the front, forms an equilateral triangle with soft edges. The cheeks as quite round in females and can be more developed in males, though in a reasonable proportion if compared to the general structure of the cat. In profile, the skull and the forehead are slightly rounded and prolonged by a harmonious convex curve reaching above the eyes, and a slight gradual concave curve under them.

Of medium length, neither pointed nor excessively rounded, the muzzle gently prolongs the triangle of the head. The chin is firm.

The eyes are oval, slightly oblique. The axis of the eyes prolongs itself towards the base of the ears. The color is the most intense blue possible.

Broad at the base and rounded at the tips, the ears are of medium size and set wide apart, so as not to alter the equilateral triangle of the head. Of medium length, the neckline is strong-muscled, especially in males.

Of semi-foreign format, the body is of medium size, very muscular but without heaviness. The chest is wide-open and slightly rounded.

Rather fine, the paws are wellproportioned if compared to the body.

The feet, oval, are of medium size.

Of medium length, thick at the base, the tail gets thinner and ends in a slightly rounded extremity.

The hair is short and thick. The fur is close-lying. Its texture is delicate and silky.

Coat

The Thaï is a colorpoint cat. There must, therefore, be a clear contrast between the color of the points, which is the most homogeneous possible, and that of the body, which is uniform. The absence of ghost marks is desired, with, however, a tolerance concerning tabby cats.

There must be taken into account the effect of age and the base color in the evolution of the colorpoint pattern: the points are often incompletely developed in the kitten, especially as regards the diluted tints, whilst the darker shades on the body of a mature cat are normal.

E – BREEDS BOTH MEDIUM-LONG HAIR AND SHORT HAIR UNDER 2 NAMES

ABYSSINIAN
ASIAN
ENGLISH BURMESE
BURMILLA
CORNISH REX
MANX
EGYPTIAN MAU
ORIENTAL
RUSSIAN
SIAMESE
SCOTTISH FOLD
SCOTTISH STRAIGHT

The correspondences between breeds

PERSIAN (LH)	EXOTIC SHORTHAIR (SH)
ABYSSINIAN (SH)	SOMALI (MLH)
ASIAN (SH)	TIFFANY (MLH)
BURMESE ANGLAIS (SH)	TIFFANY (MLH)
BURMILLA (SH)	TIFFANY (MLH)
CORNISH REX (SH)	CALIFORNIAN REX (MLH)
MANX (SH)	CYMRIC (MLH)
EGYPTIAN MAU (SH)	SHIRAZI (MLH)
ORIENTAL (SH)	MANDARIN (MLH)
RUSSIAN (SH)	NEBELUNG (MLH)
SIAMESE (SH)	BALINAIS (MLH)
SCOTTISH FOLD (SH)	HIGHLAND FOLD (MLH)
SCOTTISH STRAIGHT (SH)	HIGHLAND STRAIGHT (MLH)

ABYSSINIAN AND SOMALI

Photo Didier Hallépée

History

In the nineteenth century, a British officer of the Army of India joined his new assignment in Abyssinia (Ethiopia nowadays) with his she-cat, Zulma. Another officer, marshal Robert Napier, fell in love with this cat and brought it to England in 1868. The originality of its mantle was very much appreciated and Zulma was at the origin of a new breed called Abyssinian, in homage to the region where it came from before reaching England. Along with the Persian and the British, it is one of the most ancient recognized breeds.

Later on, an English lady travelled around Abyssinia looking for authentic Abyssinian cats. She found none, and no wonder.

The typical mantle of the Abyssinian recalls that of a hare: each hair has two or three stripes of color: this is called ticking. According to the studies on the origins of feline breeds, it looks as if the ticking comes from some regions in south-eastern Asia.

For a long while, semi-longhair kittens appeared in the litters of Abyssinians and were systematically cast aside for lack of conformity. In 1965, an American breeder decided to create out of them a new breed, recognized in 1972 as Somali.

Photo Didier Hallépée

Temper

The Abyssinian has longer back legs which give it an inimitable feline harmony. Its very feline look makes it a favourite with the public. The nose is surrounded by a fascinating edge and the face has a magnificent make-up around the eyes and on the forehead. Muscular, sportive, very affectionate, it does not mewbut coos.

Speedy, greedy, curious (be careful: it runs away!), climbing everywhere, it's a very lively companion (not to be recommended to those who mistake a cat with a decorative object), with a regal look. Medium-shaped, males are proportionally bigger than females.

Even though muscular, the Abyssinian and the Somali are agile and supple like panthers and show a great interest in what is around them. Their ticketed mantle has a quality which reflects light. Owing to the length of its hair, the Somali may look somewhat heavier than it is in reality.

Its greediness could make it obese, but its never-ending energy allows it to keep the slenderness which makes it so charming.

Standard

Shaped like a smooth triangle, the head has a rounded outline without any straight line, seen both from the front and from the side. The contour is a succession of very gentle curves: slightly rounded skull, slightly convex forehead, gentle hollow slope between the forehead and the nose, without an interruption. The nose must not be too long. A slight bulge , providing it does not create a too marked interruption or curve, is not at all a fault. The length of the head must be proportioned to the rest of the body. The head stands proudly on an elegant neck.

Photo bonsai-ka

en from the front as well as from the side, the muzzle has slightly rounded contours. It is neither angular, nor pinched. The chin is full. Forming gentle curves, it is neither receding nor protruding. Flabby chops are allowed in adult males. The truffle is surrounded by a line in harmony with the color of the base. The lips, too, must be pigmented with the same color.

The eyes are big, brilliant and expressive. Almond-shaped, their opening is neither oriental nor round. The colors allowed range from yellow to hazel through all the shades of green, provided their color is uniform. The eyes are underlined by a touch of "Cleopatra-like" make-up, with the same color as the base of the mantle, the make-up itself being encircled by a more clearly colored zone. Above each eye, a short vertical line, similar to a pencil mark, interrupts this clear zone.

Big, vigilant and moderately sharp, the ears are cup-shaped with a widened base. Pointing forwards, they are oriented as if the cat was listening. Moderately spaced out, in such a way that the ears are neither parallel nor vertical, their inferior hang point must be low enough, less so, however, than in the "oriental" type of cats. The hair on the ears is short and recumbent, if possible with some tipping. In the Somali, the interior of the ears is very bushy. The thumb print typical of agouti cats is desirable on the external part of the ear. It is more visible in dark- colored cats than in light-colored ones.

Long and graceful enough, the neck is slightly curved.

The body, of foreign format, is moderately long, flexible and pleasing to look at, with a welldeveloped muscular structure. It is firm to the touch, elegant, never bulky. The chest is slightly rounded. The ribs must never be flat. The back is slightly curved as if the cat was ready to jump.

Proportionally slim with regard to the body, the paws are long, strong-muscled and straight.

The feet are small, oval and compact. When upright, the Abyssinian and the Somali give the impression of standing on tiptoes. The color of the pads must be in accordance with the color of the base.

Fairly thick at the base, the tail is rather long, in any case proportioned to the body. It is rather pointed in the Abyssinian and tufty in the Somali.
As regards the Abyssinian, the mantle is elastic to the touch, a quality called "ductility", shining and thin. Short, it must in any case have a sufficient length to allow each hair to have at least four bands, alternately clear and dark, called ticking. The mantle, spread all over the body, is longer on the spine, getting gradually shorter on the head, sides and legs. Without being woolly, the down-hair accounts partly for the specificity of the Abyssinian, silky and elastic at times.

As far as the Somali is concerned, the mantle is semi-long, and rather close-lying . It is shorter on the shoulders and the spine, getting gradually longer on the sides. The collar and the rumps are quite bushy. The down-hair must not be woolly.

Authorized crossings

Abyssinian x Abyssinian
Somali x Somali
Abyssinian x Somali.

Coat

The color of their mantle is an essential quality of the Abyssinian and the Somali. It must not be drab, in any case, but, on the contrary, as contrasted as possible. To this end, the mantle of the Abyssinian and the Somali seems to be provided with a shining quality which reinforces the intensity of its color. Each hair must have at least four bands, alternately clear and dark, called ticking, except for the hair on the belly, chest, neck, interior of paws, and under the tail, which is not ticked. The pigmentation of these zones must, however, be homogeneous. When looked at from the skin to the tip, the ticked hair must begin with a clear band and end (distal part) with a dark one. The Abyssinian and the Somali being tabby cats, their chin and the upper part of their throat are of a paler color, ivory rather than white.

Let us note a band of darker color on the spine and the tail, heightening the feral "look" of the Abyssinian and the Somali. The "soles", that is a darker coloration on the backside of the legs, are appreciated.

The four traditional colors of the Abyssinian are hare (warm brown hair with black-brown ticking, apricot down-hair tabby ticked), sorrel (red-copper hair with red-brown ticking, apricot-cinnamon tabby ticked), blue (grey hair with steelgrey blue ticking, cream down-hair), and fawn (beige hair with dark cream ticking, down-hair pale cream).

The introduction of gene I permitted the creation of an Abyssinian with a silvery mantle, the Abyssinian Silver. The pattern is the same as for nonsilver cats, but the paler color between the bands on the base color is replaced with the most silvery shade possible. The reddish shadows, called "rufus", even if not desired, must not be too heavily penalized, especially if they are located along the spine.

Nowadays, the Abyssinian is accepted in all colors, only in tabby ticked pattern.

ENGLISH BURMESE, ASIAN, BURMILLA & TIFFANY

Photo Earth68

History

Burmese means Burman in English. In spite of this, this breed has nothing to do with the Birman which nowadays is called Sacred Cat of Burma in order to avoid such confusion. The first Burmese came from Wong Mau, a she-cat carried to the USA in 1930 by Joseph Thompson, a medical officer. This cat is supposed to have resulted from the crossing of golden-eyed Siamese and darkcolored cats. Crossed with darkcolored Siamese, she permitted getting cats with a unique color, sepia. This new breed was immediately recognized in the USA.

This origin accounts for a rather strong resemblance between Burmese and Siamese at that time, the main difference being the color as gene c_s of the Siamese (colorpoint pattern – only the extremities are colored) is replaced with gene c_b of the Burmese (pattern sepia – attenuation of the color on the body except for the extremities).

With the evolution of tastes, breeders caused the morphology of cats to evolve. The Siamese has become much more long-limbed, the traditional Siamese being renamed Thai. As for the Burmese, it has evolved on the one hand towards the Burmese called American (cat of cobby format), on the other hand towards the Burmese called British (cat of semi-foreign format). These two cats have nowadays sufficiently different morphologies to be considered as different breeds.

Photo David Johnson

In the USA, during the seventies, some crossings between Persians permitted the creation of a semi-long variety. This variety was named Tiffany. In Great Britain, it is also called Chantilly.

In 1981, Baroness Miranda von Kirchberg crossed the Burmese with other breeds in order to get other colors. In particular, the utilization of a Chinchilla Persian allowed obtaining the golden and silvershaded colors.

The classical colored cats were named Asian. The golden or silver-shaded cats were named Burmilla (BURmese ChinchILLA).

Temper

The Burmese is a cat with a stable loving character (at times it is even nicknamed "cat-dog"), full of energy, very playful and extremely captivating. It is very extroverted and has a strong personality.

It is defined as talkative, with a sweeter voice than the Siamese.

Photo Scotia

Standard

Mediumsized. A front view of the head shows a short triangle, broad at the level of the cheek-bones and ending in a spindle with a slightly rounded muzzle. The upper side of the skull is wide and slightly convex. The forehead is slightly rounded. The nose has a clear stop and then ends in a straight line.

The top of the nose and the chin form a straight vertical line. The lower jaw : is quite thick at the chin. A slight pinch is admitted in kittens.

Big, the eyes are set wide apart. The upper line of them is bent, slanting slightly towards the nose. The lower line is rounded. The color is particularly bright and shining. With the British Burmese, all nuances from yellow to amber are accepted, golden yellow being the preferred one. With the Asian and the Burmilla, all nuances from yellow to green are accepted; gold is preferred with the solid cats and green with the silver ones. With the Tiffany, the color of the eyes is related to the pattern of the coat. The shape, size and location of the eyes are more important than their color. The color of the eyes is very sensitive to the variations in the intensity and tonality of the light. If possible: assessment is to be made in the daylight.

Of medium size, the ears are set wide apart on a slightly rounded skull and ideally on the extension of the triangle formed by the head. Wide at the base, their extremity is rounded. Seen from the side, they are slightly pointed forward. The ears may seem proportionally bigger in kittens than in adults and smaller in males with well-developed chops.

The neck is muscular and of medium size.

Of semi-foreign format, the body is of average length and size, firm and muscular to the touch, and heavier than it seems. The chest is strong and rounded in profile. The back is straight.

Somewhat thin, the paws are proportioned to the body. The back ones are slightly higher than the front ones.

The feet are oval and finely chiseled .

Fairly thick at the base, the tail tapers and ends in a rounded tip. Of average length, it reaches the shoulders when stretching along the body.

In the Asian, the British Burmese and the Burmilla the coat is almost without an undercoat, short, thin, bright like silk when touched and well distributed all over the body.

In the Tiffany, the semi-long coat is silky and thin with little undercoat. Bright, it is longer at the level of the collar, the rumps, under the belly and on the tail.

Authorized crossings

All between Asian, British Burmese, Burmilla and Tiffany.

Coat

In sepia cats, the color of the coat is more marked towards the extremities of the paws, the tail, the mask and the ears, which are darker. Tolerances are accepted for the color and the pattern of the coat in kittens and young cats.

Asian

All colors but white, traditional pattern.

British Burmese

All colors, sepia pattern

Burmilla

All colors, traditional or sepia pattern, goldenshaded, golden shell, silver-shaded and chinchilla only motifs.

Tiffany

All colors, patterns and motifs admitted for the Asian, the Burmese and the Burmilla.

CORNISH REX & CALIFORNIAN REX

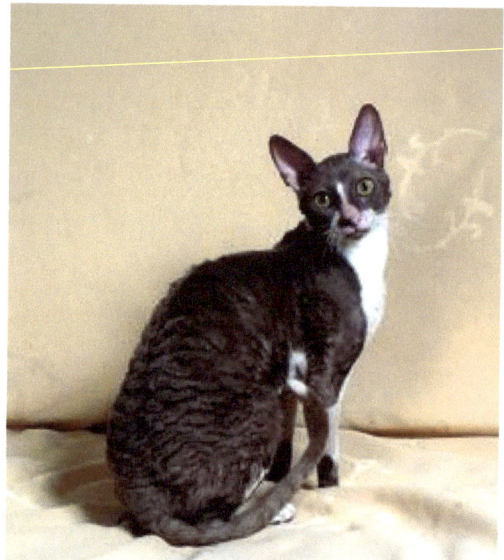

Photo Gerver

History

The Cornish Rex, also known as Cornwall Rex, is characterized by his soft and notched shorthaired coat.

He is a native of Great Britain and is the result of a spontaneous mutation which occurred in 1950 in Cornwall. His name first evokes his hometown, second the Rex rabbit fur his coat looks like.

The breed was recognized in 1967.

The longhaired Rex variety is called Californian. It appeared in the 1960s in California. The Californian Rex is recognized as a new breed and therefore cannot participate in championships.

Temper

The specific aspect of the Cornish Rex coat is due to the recessive form of R gene, responsible for the absence of awn hair. His guard hair is short and wavy.

The Cornish Rex is a very sociable cat who hates loneliness. He enjoys the company of other cats and dogs. He is lively, bustling, and very playful, affectionate and sensitive, always looking for hugs and attention.

The Cornish Rex is also very talkative and speaks in a shrill voice. He is usually very much attached to his master and is truly "glue-like". He hates exposure to cold.

Photo Paul Lewis

Standard

Longer than wide, the head is medium in size. From the side, one clearly sees two distinct curved lines. The first one goes from top of head to nose bridge. The second one goes from that point to the end of the nose. These lines form two characteristic concave arches called "Roman nose".

The skull is eggshaped, which is emphasized by the prominent occiput. The nose is broad and rounded.

The whisker pads are full and clearly defined, forming a slight pinch. The chin continues the oval of the head.

Oval and wide open, the eyes are medium, slanted and set about one eye's width apart. Eye color should be related to coat color.

Large, set high on the head, the ears are cone-shaped.

Long, slender and muscular, the neck has a characteristic arched shape.

Oriental in type, the body is long with a full deep rib cage and an arched back resembling that of a greyhound. The hindquarters are slightly rounded and strong-muscled. The bone structure is delicate.

Tall and slender, the legs are firm and muscular.

Oval, the feet are small. The Cornish Rex and the Californian Rex seem to be standing on their toes like dancers.

Long and whip-like, the tail is covered with a fine and, if possible, wavy fur.

Cornish Rex: short and very soft to the touch, the coat is wavy, forming successive astrakhan-like waves. There should be whiskers, though short and often broken.

Californian Rex: semi-long and very soft to the touch, the coat is curly with wavy hair tufts. The whiskers are long and flexible.

The coat of the Cornish Rex and Californian Rex is made up of guard hair, so modified that it looks like down, and of an undercoat. There is no awn hair between guard hair and undercoat. The fur is shorter and denser on legs and head.

The Cornish Rex and the Californian Rex combine natural elegance and athletic musculature.

Authorized crossings

Cornish Rex x Cornish Rex
Cornish Rex x Californian Rex
Californian Rex x Californian Rex

Coat

All colors

MANX & CYMRIC

Photo Wikipedia

History

The Manx or cat of the Isle of Man is a natural breed from the Isle of Man. His essential characteristic is to be a tailless cat.

This breed originated from a genetic mutation resulting from inbreeding due itself to the island isolation. He was presented at the first cat show at Crystal Palace in 1871.

According to legend, the Manx was the last animal to climb onto the Ark of Noah, but when he boarded it, the ship's door just closed on his tail which thus got severed.

A more modern legend says that the inhabitants of the island, during a severe winter, cut off the tails of all their cats to save firewood. So they could close their front door more quickly on the entrance of a cat, saving a little heat and therefore firewood.

The Cymric (from Welsh Cymru, meaning Wales) is the longhair variety of Manx. His origin is natural and was recognized in 1970.

Temper

The lack of tail is due to:

- Ml polygenes that prevent full development of the spinal cord, so conditioning the length of the tail.
- A specific dominant M gene that allows the expression of Ml polygenes.

Depending on the quantity of Ml polygenes, the Manx's tail will be more or less short. Thus, there are different varieties:

- Rumpy: completely tailless cat;
- Rumpy riser: a bulge of 1 to 3 sacral vertebrae;
- Stumpy: a bulge of 1 to 3 caudal vertebrae;
- Longy: the tail is normal.

The Longy is not accepted at shows.

In homozygotous cats (MM), the development of the spine is insufficient, the cat is not viable and die in utero.

The crossing of two Rumpi cats causes an insufficient rate of polygenes. The development of the spine is insufficient, the cat is not viable and dies in utero.

The Manx is heterozygotous with M gene, a crossover Manx X m Manx gives only 66% of kittens without a tail. Considering the problems with the rumpy Manx, marriages with other races are allowed, but only 50% of kittens will be without a tail. (These percentages are probabilities, of course)

The Manx cat is easygoing, affectionate and adapts well to changes. He's a tough cat and a good hunter.

Standard

The head is broad with wellrounded contours when viewed from any angle. The cheeks are full. The top of the head is rounded, continued by a slightly concave curve. The nose is short and broad. A slight stop is allowed. Adult males have powerful jowls.

When viewed from the front or from the side, the muzzle is set in a clearly defined circle with firm and full whisker pads. The nose and edge of the nose are straight. The end of the nose is in line with the very firm chin.

Round, big and wide-open, the eyes are set wide apart, which strengthens the breadth of the nose. The eye color should be uniform and in relation to coat color. The more intense and brilliant tones are preferred.

Wide at the base, the ears are medium to small, with rounded tips. They are set wide apart and should fit into the rounded contours of the head.

Stocky and muscular, the neck is very short, almost non-existent.

Cobby in type, the body is compact, thick, muscular, strong and well-rounded. The back forms a smooth continuous arch from the shoulders to the well-rounded rump. The bone structure is strong, with a powerful musculature. The size of the body is medium to large.

Medium, legs are slightly shorter than the body. Bone frame is sturdy and they are strongly muscled.

The feet are round and firm.

The Manx is tailless. No penalty should be given for a slight bulge of cartilage if it does not stop the judge's hand when its palm is stroking the cat down its back and over its rump.

Manx: short, dense and thick fur, straight to such an extent that it stands away from the neck when the cat moves its head. It looks like a woolen carpet. The coat has a thick undercoat and gives the impression of a good natural protection.

Cymric: semilong, silky fur, with a thick undercoat. Ruff and britches are richly furnished with hair.

Authorized crossings

Manx X Manx
Manx X Cymric
Cymric X Cymric
Manx X British Shorthair and Longhair

Cymrix X British Shorthair and Longhair

Rumpy, rumpy riser and stumpy Manx (or Cymric) can be married only to longy Manx (or Cymric).

Coat

All colors

EGYPTIAN MAU & SHIRAZI

Photo Didier Hallépée

History

By the beginning of the twentieth century, Italy was populated by the descendants of the Egyptian cat. According to descriptions, a large number of them were cats with spotted hair resembling the pharaoh's cats.

Due to the Second World War, many cats died in Italy and the direct descendants of the pharaoh's cats had practically disappeared. Nevertheless, spotted cats are still found in Italy, and, as the story goes, also in Provence. In the movie "The Horseman on the Roof" (1994 – Jean-Paul Rappeneau), the feline hero has all the characteristics of the bronze Mau.

On the contrary, the brown cat spotted with black seems to be still rather common in North Africa. Road cats looking like the bronze Mau have been spotted as far away as Morocco. On the other side of Egypt, this kind of cat can also be found all along the Silk Road.

Nathalie Troubetzkoï was an exiled Russian princess led to live in Rome by the vicissitudes of life. Nathalie was really fond of cats. One day, a young boy brought her a kitten inside a carton. The unusual beauty of this kitten did conquer her heart at once. The kitten was named Ludivine and nicknamed Ludol or Lulu. Lulu had a beautiful silver coat with black spots. The princess noticed that the box which had contained the kitten was coming from Egypt. It was in this way that she deduced the origin of this wonderful cat. She quickly understood that she had met a descendant of the cats of the Pharaoh.

Photo Didier Hallépée

She alerted her numerous friends, asking them to find for her another cat of this type in order to get newborns with the same look. Some friends found Gregorio for her, a black male, 11 years old, coming from a spotted family. Her friend, the ambassador of Syria, brought her an authentic specimen from the Near East, Geppa, a black smoke male.

Lulu and Geppa soon gave birth to the first brood (1953), which was similarly spotted as their parents. Among them, Nathalie Troubetzkoï selected and kept a small silver female, Baba. Later on, Gregorio made Baba pregnant with some magnificent kittens, also spotted (1953), together with, in between, a cat with a new color, Jojo, a bronze.

Nathalie Troubetzkoï began to make her cats known in Italy and went on getting them reproduced. Liza (or Donna Lisa) was presented at a show in Rome in 1955.

In 1956, she was, at last, authorized to emigrate to the USA.

As she could not take all her cats with her, she had to choose three of them and found a home for the others. Thus it was that Baba, Jojo and Liza left Italy for the conquest of the United States.

Once installed over there, Nathalie Troubetzkoï went on promoting the Egyptian cats, showing them and introducing them as a breed under the name of Egyptian Maus.

She created her own cattery under the name of Fatima cat house. In 1957, Baba was the first specimen of the race to be crowned a champion. All bred Egyptian Maus descend from the Maus of the princess.

Photo Didier Hallépée

To breed a race starting from 3 original specimens is not an easy thing. Consequently, for several years, the breeding of the Egyptian Mau had to tackle the consanguinity problems in spite of a few external contributions.

In order to find a final solution to the consanguinity problems, Didier and Marie-Christine Hallépée reintroduced specimens coming directly from Cairo: Sahourê, Otta and Maslama, which made it possible to keep the natural beauty and the endearing personality of the Mau while giving it at the same time the best robustness and health possible. All the progenies present in France take advantage of these contributions, which are found also in several foreign parentages.

Since the fifties, the British have been seduced by the Maus. Limited in their imports of these cats by quarantine rules, they tried to "recreate" the race starting from hybrids of Abyssinians, tabbies and Siamese cats.

Initially, these cats were called Maus, but they were finally recognized as a specific eastern variety: the Oriental spotted tabby.

That is why in some badly informed texts, we can at times read that the Mau descends from the Siamese and that the morphologies of both cats are alike. Some errors are hard to pass away…

Photo Didier Hallépée

Temper

The Egyptian Mau is often described as a cat-dog. It is really "sticky", does not hesitate to follow you close on your heels as you go about your house chores.

Breakfast is a very interesting activity: after a long night, at last you are available for the so much longed-for endearment session. This adorable Mau cat will then climb on to your knees and will rub against your arm which, at the same time, will desperately be trying to control the path described by your cup of nice and warm coffee!

In the evening, while watching TV, you will suddenly realize that it is lying there, dozing on your knees without your being aware of it!

Often, it looks at you and with its eyes it can transmit many messages. It does not mew too noisily, but modulates its voice and is able to express many things.

Some progenies are shyer than others. These shy cats have a tendency to run away from those they do not recognize as members of the family. They are often cats belonging to one person only. When a visitor is present, they move to another room or hide under a piece of furniture. They are not attracted by vast spaces: they prefer the reassuring smallness of home.

It is in the quietness of the evening that even the most timid come up and lie on their master's bed and finally get their caresses.

Such cats are not there to attract the admiration of visitors. They are there to give true affection to the master who deserves it.

Compared to the Abyssinian, the Mau is quite calm in the kitchen! Let's be fair: they are not all greedy; but a good part of them – which cannot be ignored – is really interested in what is going on there and is keen to run some risks to improve their everyday meal.

Photo Didier Hallépée

It is not a fuzz-ball! When playing or trying to escape from you (no, mum, you will not give me my medicines!), it is almost impossible to catch it. Under its belly, there is a piece of skin hanging down, the belly flap.

This flap allows the cat to stretch out better when running or jumping. In this way, it can jump over more than two meters or run at more than 50

km/h. Well, not all of them: when the pocket is quite full, the cat loses its agility...
The Mau has a very strong personality though it is very affectionate, a little shy or semi-savage (like those living free in Egypt).

A relationship made up of affection and respect settles between the two of you. Impossible to ignore it or its desires. The Mau in need of caresses will not stop until it gets them.

The Mau requiring respect for its tranquility, will be able to convince you that you do have a right to get close, talk, have a personalized approach but not the right to touch it and it will assume an indignant countenance if the status quo is not respected.

As for the cat who has chosen to love you above anyone else, when the time of hated care comes, it will wriggle, scream, show it could defend itself... and will avoid causing any harm to you!

There is also the little savage born in Egypt which has adopted you. Its presence and affection are such that you have to exert an effort to keep in mind you cannot hold it in your arms.

Finally, there is the quiet one: its personality is a relaxing one. It lies against cats, dogs and humans and calms down even the most excited of them.

The cat is already known for being an animal with a strongly expressive personality. This is a particularly remarkable feature of the Mau.

Photo Didier Hallépée

Standard

The Egyptian Mau is a naturally spotted race of domestic cats.

This mid-size cat, which combines power and elegance, is impressive for the surprising contrast of its short glossy mantle and for the expression of its bright green eyes.

Medium-sized, the head forms a triangle with a soft outline without a single even plane. Seen from the front, the cheeks are level, but in males flabby cheeks are accepted. The nose has the same width over its whole length.

Seen from the side, the forehead is slightly rounded and prolonged by a slight concave slant at the level of the eyes. The nose is straight. Neither short nor long, the muzzle, all gentle curves, completes the triangle of the head. The chin is solid, neither protuberant nor receding.

Almond-shaped, the eyes are big and wide-open, slightly askew but not oriental. The best color is called "gooseberry green".

Photo Didier Hallépée

Medium to big in size, the ears are wide at the base, rounded at the tip and set rather wide apart on the extension of the lines formed by the head. Seen from the side, they are situated rather backward.

The exterior of the ears is covered with a very short fur, whilst the interior, pale pink, is almost transparent.

The neckline is bent, wellmarked.

Of semi-foreign type, the body, of medium size, is a harmonious combination of power and elegance.

The shoulders jut out, and their angle is easily perceived.

The muscles are welldeveloped, especially in adult males, which can be more square-built than females.

Between the back limbs, the typical ventral pocket is required.

Of medium size, the limbs have a moderate bone framework and a strong musculature.

The back limbs, taller than the fore ones, grant a particular balance to the Egyptian Mau which, when standing erect, seems to stand on tiptoes. Small and delicate, the feet are slightly oval, almost rounded.

Of medium size, the tail is somewhat thick at the base and then gets thinner towards its extremity.

Short, the fur must in any case have a sufficient length to allow each single hair (in the spotted zones) to have at least four bands, alternately clear and dark. It is well distributed along the body.

In the silver and the bronze, it is gentle and elastic to the touch. In the black smoke and the black, it is thinner and silky.

Photo Didier Hallépée

The spotted tabby patron alone is accepted. There must be a good contrast between the pale color of the background of the hair and the marks of the deepest color.

The forehead has the characteristic "M" of tabbies, and the eye, the typical Egyptian makeup. A second line situated under the makeup fades away towards the ear.

Some welmarked straight lines originate from the M on the skull, reach across the neck and become wellaligned spots on the spine.

The marks are wider on the shoulders, thus making the transition between the lines and the spots. The rest of the body is covered with dots of variable size and form, but never in a line to avoid recalling the mackerel tabby pattern. The neck is decorated by at least one open collar and the belly has a few spots aligned like "button vests".

The limbs often have some thick rings, which can be different and open. The tail, too, has rings, with a black tip except for the bronze, whose tip can range from dark brown to black.

Coat

Silver
Silver base, pale and luminous, contrasting with the black dots. The back of the ears is greyish pink with black points. The nose, lips and eyes are underlined in black. The throat, chin and nostrils are silver, almost white. The truffle is brickred. The pads are black with some black also around the toes and the heels.

Bronze
Bronze base, brilliant, fading from chamois to ivory under the belly, darker on the hind limbs and contrasting with black or dark brown dots. A grey undercoat is accepted. The back of the ears is pink fawn with dark brown to black points. The throat, chin and nostrils range from cream white to beige. The truffle is brown red. The pads are dark brown to black with the same color between the toes and the back of the rear limbs. According to some standards, the Egyptian Mau can be more or less of a copper tint.

Black smoke (Pewter)
Even if not sharp, the black smoke color in the Egyptian Mau must allow the spotted tabby patron (ghost marks) to express itself clearly. The base of the hair is bright silver for a quarter of its length; the remaining three quarters are anthracitegray. The colored dots on the three quarters of the hair are black and thus they contrast with the rest of the mantle. The throat, chin and nostrils are lighter-coloured. The nose, lips and eyes are underlined in black. The truffle and the pads are black, with some black around the toes and on the back of the rear limbs.

Black
Even if not sharp, the black color of the Egyptian Mau can allow the spotted tabby (ghost marks) patron to express itself. The hair is bright over its whole length.

Blue
The blue color is recognized solely in CFA in its four varieties (blue silver, blue self, blue smoke, blue solid).

Shirazi
The longhaired Mau, bred under the name of Shirazi, is not recognized.

RUSSIAN BLUE & NEBELUNG

Photo Ruskis

History

The Russian cat is also known under the names Russian Blue, Arkhangelsk Blue or Maltese Cat.

The first known specimens in England reached Great Britain coming from Arkhangelsk, Russia, hence the names Arkhangelsk Cat, Archangel, Archangel Blue they got by that time. Some of them were shown at the first feline show at Crystal Palace in 1871, in a class reserved to blue cats. From that show onwards people could see longhaired specimens.

According to some theories, this cat should be native to the Mediterranean Basin, like the Chartreux. From there, it may have gone eastwards to Russia where it was appreciated as a companion animal and hunted for its warm fur, and westwards to Malta and Spain, which earned it the names Maltese cat or Blue Spanish. It was anyway under the name Maltese cat that it appeared in France in 1925.

The breed got the name Russian Blue in 1939.

With the Second World War, the breeding of the Russian Cat disappeared almost completely from Europe. As for the longhaired variety, it was almost forgotten.

The breeding of the Russian Blue re-appeared in the sixties, when some crossings with the Siamese were tried out before they were forbidden in 1965 and before the breed did stabilize. It was also during the sixties that the breed became popular in the USA.

In 1984, in the USA, Sarah Cobb recreated the longhaired variety of the Russian Blue, which got the name Nebelung (creator of mist). Exchange with Russia permitted enrichment of the genetic pool. Furthermore, it then happened that the very rare Russian Blues were carriers of the recessive gene responsible for the semi-long hair, and this was also a precious contribution.

Finally, the lovers of the unexpected were able to get the black Russian as well as the blue and the white ones recognized. Consequently, the breed was renamed Russian, the name Russian Blue being reserved for the blue specimens.

Temper

The Russian Blue is characterized by its thick fluffy mantle of a silver blue color and by its green eyes.

The Russian Blue has a bright intelligence, is very affectionate, playful, calm and quiet with a sweet melodious mewing. It is very affectionate to its master with whom it can live a true love story. It is a charming companion, careful and sociable with other animals, often shy with strangers.

It is a timid cat which loves comfort and tranquility and needs a calm serene habitat. It needs, therefore, to be reassured when attending a show.

It is a playful cat, active when it wishes to be so, never restless. The male cares for its kittens and at times replaces the mother in watching over them.

Photo Wikipedia

Standard

The shape of the head is due to seven plain faces which are as follows: from above the skull to the forehead; from there down to the tip of the nose, which, if seen in profile, forms a straight line; from the tip of the nose down to the extremity of the chin; two symmetrical faces on each side of the muzzle; two symmetrical ones formed by the broad high cheek-bones. Triangular, when seen from the front, the head is particularly wide at the level of the eyes.

With its rounded outline, on the other hand, the rather short muzzle without a pinch prolongs the triangle of the head. The slightly raised corners of the mouth give a sweet, smiling-like expression.

Nut-shaped, the eyes are rather big and set wide apart. In adults, the color is the most intense green possible.

As high as wide at the base, the ears are spaced out the width of one ear. Externally covered with short thin hair, they are furnished with longer hair on half of the internal surface.

The neckline, long and thin, looks heavier than it really is, due to the thickness of the fur.

The body, of foreign format, is long and elegant. Strong-muscled and without any heaviness, it may seem more robust than it is in reality, this being due to the thickness of the fur, especially in the Nebelung. The bone-framework is thin and the musculature powerful.

Long and thin, the paws are proportioned to the body. The feet are small and somewhat round.

Rather thick at the base, the tail is of medium length, reaching the base of the scapulae. In the Russian, the tail gets thinner towards its sharp extremity. In the Nebelung, the tail is furnished with abundant hair.

In the Russian, the mantle is short, thin and soft due to the importance of its down-hair.

In the Nebelung: the fur is of medium length, formed by rather thin down-hair covered by thicker guard hair. Males often do have a nice collaret, more unobtrusive in females. Culottes are desirable as well as light lynx tips on the back of the ears.

Authorized crossings

Russian x Russian
Russian (only blue) x Nebelung
Nebelung x Nebelung

Coat

Russian: Blue, black, white
Nebelung: Blue

Blue
Mantle of a uniform bright blue, with a preference for light tonalities. The extremity of the guard hair has a silvery coloration giving the fur a bright look, as if sprinkled with silver. The truffle is coal-grey and the pads are dark lilac.

White
White mantle with silvery reflections. The truffle and pads are pink.

Black
Brilliant coalblack mantle down to the root. The truffle and pads are black or dark brown.

SCOTTISH & HIGHLAND

Photo Steve Jurvetson

History

The Scottish Fold is characterized by its folded ears. The variety with erect ears is called Scottish Straight.

The spontaneous mutation responsible for the folded ears appeared in 1961 among some Scottish farm cats. It was discovered by William and Mary Ross, who developed this genetic particularity and gave birth to the breed of the Scottish Folds.

As the crossings went on, some semi-long subjects did appear. This variety was named Scottish Fold Longhair, Highland Fold or Coupari.

The breed was recognized in 1971.

Temper

The fold of the ears is caused by a dominant specific FD gene, whose action is probably connected with the presence of polygenes.

The action of FD gene is little known. Probably, it consists in modifications of the bone structure at the cartilage level.

And this is evidenced at the level of the ears with an insufficient cartilage structure that fails to keep the ears erect.

The action of gene FD is more or less pronounced and results in more or less folded ears. So, we can distinguish:
- the Single Fold (formerly Loose Fold) whose ears fold in their middle;
- the double fold, more appreciated in contests, whose ears are completely flattened on the head;.

In the homozygotous cats (FDFD), the action of the gene causes disabling bone deformations. Due to this, the mating of two Folds is forbidden by the standards.

So, the genotype of the Scottish Fold is FDfd and that of the Scottish Straight is fdfd. Having been fixed essentially with the British, the Scottish Fold shares the feature.

Standard

The head is broad with a wellrounded outline, whatever the point of observation is. The cheeks are full; the skull is rounded, sloping downward in a slightly concave bend. The nose is short and broad. A slight stop is admitted. Adult males have powerful jowls.

Seen both from the front and in profile, the muzzle is inscribed in a clearly defined circle, with whisker pads firm and full. The nose and its edge are straight. The tip of the nose is in a line with the chin, which is quite firm.

Round, big and wide open, the eyes are at the right distance from each other, and this accentuates the width of the nose even more. The color must be uniform and in accordance with the color of the mantle. The most intense and bright tonalities are preferred.

Wide at the base, the ears are medium to small, rounded at their tip and spaced out in such a way that they do not alter the rounded contour of the head.

In the Folds, the ears are folded forward, and can have a simple or double fold. Small wellfolded ears are preferred to bigger ones with loose folds.

In the Straights: the ears are rect.

Stocky and muscular, the neckline is so short as to appear non-existent.

Of semi-cobby format, the body is broad, thick, muscular and wellrounded. The bone structure is robust and the musculature powerful. The size is medium to big. The hindquarters must feel very soft when touched.

Mediumsized, the paws are slightly smaller than the length of the body. The bone frame is robust and the musculature is strong. Particular attention will be paid to their mobility, which must be similar to that of the other breeds.

The feet are round and firm.

Thick at the base, the tail is medium to long. It gets slightly thinner with a rounded tip. Flexible, soft, it must not be rigid. In the Highlands, it must be abundantly covered with hair and panache-like.

In the Scottish, the fur is short, thick, firm and erect to the point of opening at the neckline when the cat turns its head. It can be compared to the hair of a wool carpet. The fur has thick down-hair and gives the impression of a good natural protection.

In the Highlands, the fur is semi-long, silky, with thick down-hair. The collaret and the back are abundantly furnished with hair.

Authorized crossings

Scottish Fold x British Shorthair
Scottish Fold x British Longhair
Scottish Fold x Scottish Straight
Scottish Fold x Highland Straight
Scottish Straight x British Shorthair

Scottish Straight x British Longhair
Scottish Straight x Scottish Straight
Highland Fold x British Shorthair
Highland Fold x British Longhair
Highland Fold x Highland Straight
Highland Fold x Scottish Straight
Highland Straight x British Shorthair
Highland Straight x British Longhair
Highland Straight x Highland Straight

Unions between Folds are strictly forbidden.

The Scottish Fold and the Scottish Straight (respectively Highland Fold and Highland Straight) compete in the same class.

Coat

All colors.

SIAMESE, ORIENTAL, ORIENTAL LONGHAIR, BALINAIS

Photo Karin Langner-Bahmann

History of the Siamese

It is said that the history of the domesticated cat has its origins in ancient Egypt and that it reached Asia and settled there after having followed the Silk Road.

So, when the French and the British conquered south-east Asia, the cat had already been established there for a long time. In Siam, it was the sacred animal of the royal family.

The korat was much appreciated at the royal court of Siam. In 1884, king Rama V presented a Siamese to the United Kingdom general consul,

Edward Blencowe Gould, pretending that this cat was the symbol of Siam, so as to maintain the exclusivity of the precious korat inside his kingdom.

These cats were named Siamese and were on show at the Crystal Palace show in 1885.

By then the trend had started and during the successive years, several cats were brought over from Siam and became the very first specimens of the Siamese line in Great Britain.

In France, Auguste Pavie began the trend by bringing in himself some Siamese cats in 1885. In 1890 the Siamese found its way to the United States. Since then, Siam has become Thailand, but the Siamese keeps alive the memories of that time for us.

Photo Natasha Winborn

The first standard of the breed was published in 1892 by the GCCF and the first clubs were created in 1901.

At its origin, the true Siamese cat had a rounded head, the body was robust and its muscle structure athletic. Its hair was short and light-colored with dark extremities (head, paws and tail).

It was this difference in colors between the body and the extremities that fascinated the first collectors and characterized the breed so much as to give the name Siamese to the gene responsible for this coloration.

Many discovered the Siamese at the movies, thanks to a few animated cartoons by Walt Disney: The Lady and the Tramp (1955), adapted from a work by Ward Greene, Happy Dan, the Whistling Dog (1937).

Oriental

In the fifties, the Siamese became very common. Its constitution got finer owing to the evolution of the breeders' taste, and several colors came into existence.

The Siamese was then to generate a whole family of cats with colored extremities: the Orientals.

Balinese and Mandarin

Photo Mirjam Kessler

Such a beauty also seduced the lovers of the semi-long hair. In this way it was that the Balinese came into existence, a semi-long hair variety of the Siamese, and the Mandarin, a semi-longhaired variety of the Oriental.

Thai

Nowadays, Siamese and Orientals are elegant long-limbed cats, with thin paws and the hind-limbs slightly taller than the forelimbs.

The old Siamese with the rather rounded face was recreated under the name Thaï.

Temper

Apart from its beauty, what fascinates most in the Siamese (and its successive varieties), is its exclusive character which makes it the privileged feline companion. They say that he who has never lived with a Siamese does not really know the feline soul.

The Siamese, the Oriental, the Balinese and the Mandarin are long-limbed cats, elegant, slender and strong-muscled. Combining harmoniously a thin bone frame with a soft firm muscle structure, they are athletic cats with smooth outlines.

These cats must be perfectly balanced; the whole harmony must not be altered by the presence of an extremely isolated morphological characteristic.

They are lively and talkative, being provided with a strong personality.

Standard

Seen from the front, the head, of medium size, is long and triangular. The skull and the forehead are flat or slightly curved.

Three types of profile are accepted: perfectly straight, slightly convex, and the one with two planes in which the forehead prolongs the nose without any interruption.

The cheeks are flat. Jowls are accepted for adult males. Seen from the front, the nose blends into the triangle of the head. The tip of the nose must not be narrow.

Seen from the side, the nose is long and straight. The jaws are medium. The chin is firm, in line with the tip of the nose.

Of medium size, the eyes are orientally shaped. Almond-shaped and set wide apart, they are slanted towards the nose in harmony with the triangle of the head. The color of the eyes is the most intense possible blue in the Siamese and the Balinese, and the most intense green for the Oriental and the Mandarin. Odd eyes (green and blue) are accepted in part-colors. Odd eyes and blue eyes are accepted in white Orientals.

Big, broad at the base, set wide apart, the ears prolong the triangle of the head.

Long, thin and elegant, the neckline sets off the head from the shoulders.

Of oriental type and of medium size, the body is long, tubular and firm. When touched, it is of astonishing thickness. It is athletic and slender, with a firm and soft musculature. The shoulders and the hips have the same breadth. The bone frame is thin.

The tail is in keeping with the length of the body and the height of the paws.
Siamese and Oriental: whip-like, the long tail ends in a point.
Balinese and Mandarin: long and thin, the tail is abundant and carried lightly , like an ostrich feather.

Long and elegant, the paws are in harmony with the length of the body. Their bone frame is thin and the musculature is firm.

The feet are oval and small.

In the Siamese and the Oriental, the hair, very short, thick and shiny, is close-lying on the body. Its texture is thin and silky.

In the Balinese and the Mandarin, the hair, semi-long and thin, is silky and lies close to the body. There is practically no down-hair. The hair is shorter on the shoulders and gets longer on the sides. The back and the tail are abundantly furnished with hair. It must not have any ruff.

Neither fat nor thin, its thinness must not be mistaken with skininess.

Authorized crossings

Siamese x Siamese
Siamese x Balinese
Siamese x Oriental
Siamese x Mandarin
Balinese x Balinese
Balinese x Oriental
Balinese x Mandarin
Oriental x Oriental
Oriental x Mandarin
Mandarin x Mandarin

Coat

The Siamese
Short hair, color point.

The Oriental
Short hair, entirely colored.

The Balinese
Semi-long hair, color point.

The Mandarin
Semi-long hair, entirely colored.

The Siamese and the Balinese are color point. There must be, therefore, a clear contrast between the color of the points, which is the most homogeneous possible, and that of the body, which is uniform.
The absence of ghost marks is desirable, with, in any case, a tolerance as regards tabby cats.

What must be kept in mind is the effect of age and of the base color on the evolution of the color point pattern: the points are often not completely developed in kittens, especially as regards the diluted shades, whilst some darker shadows on the body of a mature cat are normal.

TABLE DES MATIÈRES

CLASSIFICATION OF THE BREED CATS	11
The categories	11
The notion of breed	13
The definition of breeds	16
The varieties	17
Listing of the breeds	19
Long hair category	*19*
Medium long hair category	*20*
Short hair category	*21*
The correspondences between breeds	*24*
A – LONG HAIR CATEGORY	25
PERSIAN & EXOTIC SHORTHAIR	26
History	26
Temper	27
Standard	28
Short hair variety	*29*
Authorized crossings	*30*
Coat	*30*
B – BREEDS EXCLUSIVELY WITH MEDIUM-LONG HAIR	33
TURKISH ANGORA	34
History	34
Temper	36
Standard	37
Coat	*39*

MAINE COON	**40**
History	40
Temper	41
Standard	42
Coat	*43*
NORWEGIAN	**44**
History	44
Temper	45
Standard	46
Coat	*47*
BIRMAN	**48**
History	48
Temper	49
Standard	50
Coat	*51*
SIBERIAN	**52**
History	52
Temper	53
Standard	54
Coat	*55*
TURKISH OF LAKE OF VAN	**56**
History	56
Temper	57
Standard	58
Coat	*59*
YORK CHOCOLATE	**61**

History	61
Temper	62
Standard	62
Coat	*63*
C –BREEDS BOTH WITH MEDIUM-LONG AND SHORT HAIR	**65**
AMERICAN BOBTAIL	**66**
History	66
Temper	66
Standard	67
Authorized crossings	*68*
Coat	*68*
AMERICAN CURL	**69**
History	69
Temper	70
Standard	70
Authorized crossings	*71*
Coat	*72*
BRITISH	**73**
History	73
Temper	74
Standard	74
Authorized crossings	*76*
Coat	*76*
JAPANESE BOBTAIL	**77**
History	77
Temper	78

Standard	**78**
Authorized crossings	*79*
Coat	*79*
KURILIAN BOBTAIL	**80**
History	**80**
Temper	**80**
Standard	**81**
Authorized crossings	*81*
Coat	*81*
LAPERM	**82**
History	**82**
Temper	**83**
Standard	**83**
Authorized crossings	*84*
Coat	*84*
MUNCHKIN	**85**
History	**85**
Temper	**85**
Standard	**86**
Authorized crossings	*87*
Coat	*87*
PIXIE-BOB	**88**
History	**88**
Temper	**89**
Standard	**89**
Authorized crossings	*91*
Coat	*91*

SELKIRK	**92**
History	**92**
Temper	**93**
Standard	**93**
Authorized crossings	*94*
Coat	*95*
TONKINESE	**96**
History	**96**
Temper	**97**
Standard	**97**
Authorized crossings	*98*
Coat	*98*
D – BREEDS EXCLUSIVELY WITH SHORT HAIR	**101**
AMERICAN SHORTHAIR	**102**
History	**102**
Temper	**103**
Standard	**103**
Authorized crossings	*104*
Coat	*104*
AMERICAN WIREHAIR	**105**
History	**105**
Temper	**105**
Standard	**106**
Authorized crossings	*107*
Coat	*107*
BENGAL	**108**

History	108
Temper	110
Standard	111
Coat	*113*
AMERICAN BURMESE & BOMBAY	**114**
History	114
Temper	115
Standard	116
Authorized crossings	*117*
Coat	*117*
CALIFORNIA SPANGLED	**118**
History	118
Temper	118
Standard	119
Coat	*119*
CEYLON	**120**
History	120
Temper	121
Standard	121
Coat	*122*
CHARTREUX	**123**
History	123
Temper	124
Standard	124
Coat	*125*
CHAUSIE	**126**

History	**126**
Temper	**127**
Standard	**127**
Authorized crossings	*128*
Coat	*128*
DEVON REX	**129**
History	**129**
Temper	**129**
Standard	**130**
Coat	*131*
DONSKOY	**132**
History	**132**
Temper	**132**
Standard	**133**
Coat	*134*
EUROPEAN SHORTHAIR	**135**
History	**135**
Temper	**137**
Standard	**138**
Coat	*139*
GERMAN REX	**140**
History	**140**
Temper	**141**
Standard	**141**
Authorized crossings	*142*
Coat	*142*

HAVANA BROWN — 143
- History — 143
- Temper — 144
- Standard — 144
  - *Coat* — *145*

KORAT — 146
- History — 146
- Temper — 147
- Standard — 147
  - *Coat* — *148*

OCICAT — 149
- History — 149
- Temper — 150
- Standard — 150
  - *Coat* — *151*

PETERBALD — 152
- History — 152
- Temper — 152
- Standard — 153
  - *Authorized crossings* — *155*
  - *Coat* — *155*

RAGDOLL — 156
- History — 156
- Temper — 156
- Standard — 157
  - *Coat* — *158*

SAVANNAH	**159**
History	159
Temper	160
Standard	161
Authorized crossings	*162*
Coat	*162*
SINGAPURA	**163**
History	163
Temper	164
Standard	164
Coat	*165*
SNOWSHOE	**166**
History	166
Temper	166
Standard	167
Coat	*167*
SOKOKE	**169**
History	169
Temper	170
Standard	170
Coat	*171*
SPHYNX	**172**
History	172
Standard	173
Coat	*174*
THAÏ	**175**

History	175
Temper	176
Standard	176
Coat	*177*

E – BREEDS BOTH MEDIUM-LONG HAIR AND SHORT HAIR UNDER 2 NAMES — 179

   The correspondences between breeds — *179*

ABYSSINIAN AND SOMALI — 180

History	180
Temper	181
Standard	182
Authorized crossings	*184*
Coat	*184*

ENGLISH BURMESE, ASIAN, BURMILLA & TIFFANY — 185

History	185
Temper	187
Standard	187
Authorized crossings	*189*
Coat	*189*

CORNISH REX & CALIFORNIAN REX — 190

History	190
Temper	191
Standard	191
Authorized crossings	*193*
Coat	*193*

MANX & CYMRIC — 194

History	194

Temper	**195**
Standard	**195**
Authorized crossings	*196*
Coat	*197*
EGYPTIAN MAU & SHIRAZI	**198**
History	**198**
Temper	**201**
Standard	**204**
Coat	*207*
RUSSIAN BLUE & NEBELUNG	**209**
History	**209**
Temper	**210**
Standard	**212**
Authorized crossings	*213*
Coat	*213*
SCOTTISH & HIGHLAND	**214**
History	**214**
Temper	**214**
Standard	**215**
Authorized crossings	*216*
Coat	*217*
SIAMESE, ORIENTAL, ORIENTAL LONGHAIR, BALINAIS	**218**
History of the Siamese	**218**
Oriental	**220**
Balinese and Mandarin	**220**
Thai	**221**

Temper	**221**
Standard	**221**
Authorized crossings	*223*
Coat	*223*

Découvrez le mau égyptien et son histoire dans

Le chat mau égyptien
de Didier Hallépée
aux éditions Carrefour du Net

Retrouvez les maus égyptiens et les King Charles dans

Mot à mau
Mau Mews
de Didier Hallépée
aux éditions Carrefour du Net

édition bilingue – bilingual edition

MOT À MAU
LES PENSÉES DU CHAT MAU

DIDIER HALLÉPÉE

COLLECTION Arc-en-Ciel
ANIMAUX

Retrouvez les maus égyptiens et les King Charles dans

Pensées Royales Canines
King Barks
de Didier Hallépée
aux éditions Carrefour du Net

édition bilingue – bilingual edition

PENSÉES ROYALES CANINES
LES PENSÉES DU KING CHARLES

DIDIER HALLÉPÉE

COLLECTION ARC-EN-CIEL
ANIMAUX

Et retrouvez ce qu'on dit de nos compagnons dans

CITATIONS ET PROVERBES
CHATS ET CHIENS

Par Didier HALLÉPÉE

With the invention of agriculture, the man left the nomadic state to become sedentary. But at the same time, he attracts rodents and cats with them. With the invention of the grain silo began the domestication of cats in Egypt, about 4000 years ago.

Tired of his god status, the Egyptian Mau has left the land of his ancestors to conquer the world. Alley cats and breed cats are all his worthy heirs.

This is the story of the most beautiful of the Egyptian Mau cat's children, pedigree cats, that you'll find in this book.

As a high level scientific graduate **Didier HALLÉPÉE** was not promised to feline life. The discovery of the noblest of cats, the home cat, put him on the way of breeding. His passion for the Egyptian Mau did not prevent him to mix with many breed and enjoy all such beautifulness.

This is this passion he shares with us today.

www.ingramcontent.com/pod-product-compliance
Lightning Source LLC
Chambersburg PA
CBHW042058290426
44113CB00001B/5